NEVER WORK
WITH
YOUR IDOLS

NEVER WORK
WITH
YOUR IDOLS

35 COMMANDMENTS
FOR A SUCCESSFUL CAREER
IN THE MUSIC INDUSTRY

BY GIDEON KARTING

TRANSLATED BY ANTOINETTE FAWCETT

NEVER WORK WITH YOUR IDOLS
35 commandments for a successful career in the music industry

Copyright © 2022
Gideon Karting / Outliner Books

© *Gideon Karting 2021*
Authorial copyright
© *Antoinette Fawcett 2022*
Translation copyright

Layout by: Es & Zn – Esther de Boer
Dtp: Coco Bookmedia
Support: Eva, Jonas, Nina
Photo: Ben Houdijk
Font: Logical – Edward Wathert
Titlefont: Barlow
Edition: Outliner Books

ISBN 978 90 831 4872 4
ISBN 978 90 831 4873 1 (e-book)

NUR 400 / 660
BISAC MUS004000
SH SZ 42, 43 1/3

Gideon Karting
www.gideonkarting.com

Gideon Karting has been a stalwart of the music industry for more than twenty years. He started this career as a concert billposter and in the years that followed developed into one of the Netherlands' top concert promoters. In his work for Mojo Concerts and LiveNation he promoted all the Dutch shows of a wide range of leading artists, including Lady Gaga, Adele, One Direction, Arctic Monkeys, Bruno Mars, and BTS. For many years he was also the programme director of major festivals such as Lowlands, North Sea Jazz, and Pinkpop.

Karting's insider view of the music industry, his dry sense of humour and sardonic outlook, have finally found their expression in a book: Never Work With Your Idols. Karting shares all the fruits of his experience in an amusing but practical guide, taking his readers on a journey through the music industry and all its wealth of stories. With the help of his 35 Commandments, aspiring music professionals will most certainly learn how to make a successful career in this sector. Never Work With Your Idols is essential reading for people starting out in the industry and a real nostalgia trip for seasoned insiders.

CONTENTS

CURTAIN RAISER

The word 'origin' indicates where something comes from, where something started, or its source of being or existence.

As long as you start something. Without a beginning, there's no future.

WHO IS GIDEON KARTING?

The year that Charles Bukowski's second novel, *Factotum*, saw the light of day was the same year my parents were busy creating their own factotum, their 'jack-of-all-trades'. That's me, in effect. I don't really believe in the factotum concept, i.e. that someone can actually do all kinds of different things. People like that are usually far too caught up with minor details and then they have less time to truly excel in one particular specialism. But when I start listing all the things I've ever done, I do begin to question my own belief.

I started in 1992, as a singer-songwriter, and guitarist in a grunge band. So I could buy myself a guitar I worked for weeks on end, picking cucumbers in Dutch fields and greenhouses. Because I also needed guitar strings and electric cables, and I'd got pretty sick of the sight of vegetables, I swapped picking for sticking, and got work putting up concert posters for Nighttown and Rotown, well-known music venues in my home town of Rotterdam. That job meant I could easily get into all the concerts – and then I started photographing them.

Nighttown and Rotown became my home base. Because I was interested in everything and my pay rate was low, I soon started work as a lighting technician and DJ at dance nights and concerts. It didn't take long before I started organizing those kinds of events myself, as well as designing posters and stage sets, and creating the marketing strategies. My band folded, but the photography continued, which meant I could go to all the important shows and festivals in the country, as an assistant photographer for the Dutch national newspaper *De Telegraaf*, among others. For years I was there, behind the scenes and in front, at every venue and every festival.

At night I was at gigs, while in the daytime I was studying to be a creative artist. But once I'd graduated from Art School, it was high time to start specializing. In 1999 I became Rotown's local promoter, but with jobs on the side as well: running my own record label and organizing a festival.

After four years of promoting at a local level, the next step seemed obvious: I became a booker for Mojo Concerts, the biggest live music organizer in the Netherlands. It's a subsidiary of Live Nation, the biggest live music organizer in the world. The first year I just booked local artists. After that I was allowed to work with international talent. I booked the very first shows in the Netherlands of Lady Gaga, Michael Kiwanuka, Katy Perry, Bruno Mars, One Direction, BTS, Imagine Dragons, Arctic Monkeys, Tame Impala, The Kooks, Triggerfinger, The Script, Adele, Mumford & Sons, The Kyteman Orchestra, and many others. Fantastic! And I programmed entire festivals, like North Sea Jazz, Pinkpop and Lowlands. Wow! My side-lines were now part of my work, and I had complete carte blanche. At that time I was the director of two festivals, TMF Smash and Songbird. I compiled albums and organized, directed and devised shows. I made books and statues, set up a new record label, and entered the world of podcasts. And now I'm once again doing what I graduated in: making creative art. I've stopped working for the concert promoter for the time being, but that certainly doesn't mean that I've finished with the music industry. In fact, I have now started my own artist management company.

Because the common factor has always been music. During the past few decades I've immersed myself in the world we call 'the music industry' – a closed world that may look adventurous and exciting to the outsider, but may also be difficult to understand. That applies to many sectors and professions, of course. You'll get beginners there too, with no understanding of what's going on, whose clumsy actions simply make work for others. Because you can always spot these people and their actions a mile off, I'd really like to take the initiative here and offer the fruits of all my experience.

If this book means that the failures of the future will take a different path, that will be a win for the entire music industry. And if the real go-getters can get enough ammunition from this book to blaze their own trail in the industry, then it will definitely have hit its mark. And so much the better if you can see some humour in it too.

Come through this book with me as if you were going to a concert. In Part One, 'The Arena', we'll explore the playing field. Who can you find in the music industry? What do these people do, and why? What exactly is their work? What do they earn? Where can you find them? Where should or shouldn't you be?

In Part Two I focus on the artist. What exactly are artists, and what types and flavours can you find? What is their position in the industry? What does an artist do? How should you deal with them, and what benefits do they bring?

Next comes 'The Act', which is all about the tricks of the music industry trade. What steps should you take to make progress? Which rules should you follow if you want to be of added value inside it? What can you do, and what shouldn't you do at all?

In Part Four, 'The Action', we'll take a look at what you need to remember to survive in the music industry. Here I'll zoom in on all the ups and downs, and especially on the downs of doing things by trial and error!

And naturally I'll finish with an encore.

PART 1

THE ARENA

The music industry is the industry involved in the creation, performance, promotion and preservation of music.

Who are the people involved? What do they do, and why? How much do they earn? And where exactly can you find them?

THE PYRAMID

In the beginning there was nothing at all, except sand, flint and dry branches. And there was a small village called Witteon, somewhere in the Eastern Sahara. The villagers were simply dressed, in garments made of jute and with brown leather sandals. There was always an open fire burning there, with a few guys round it, who were always beating their drums. The village oddball would be there as well, leaning against a date palm and strumming his lute, while his wife played her flute every day to her heart's content.

One day a minstrel suddenly appeared from the desert sands. He wore brightly coloured clothing and had a drum on his back and bells round his arms and legs. He had a pig-gut belt around his waist, with a guitar dangling from it. He carried a silver trumpet in one hand, and was a strong, well-built man. It was the first time he had come to the village, and his music made such a racket that the villagers threatened to tar and feather him and send him back into the desert. But the village chief forbade them to do so. He thought the music was fantastic and felt that the villagers really needed proper live entertainment. It would just take some time for them to get used to it. So he made a deal with the minstrel. They would welcome him to the village once a month and in return the minstrel could pass his cap around. The more coins there were in the cap, the more frequently he could visit.

Six months passed and the minstrel had come by every month, hoping to convince the villagers of the quality of his ballads, and at last they started to recognize some of the melodies. After nine months, they even started to look forward to the minstrel's arrival. His visits were the talk of the day, not only in Witteon, but in all the surrounding villages. Rumour had it that people were actually saving up so that the minstrel would visit them more often.

Then the daughter of the village chief made another deal with the minstrel. If he would play in Witteon and the three neighbouring villages once a fortnight, he'd receive a fixed sum of cash, in ducats. In addition, the lute player and his wife were given the right to play his tunes. The minstrel signed at once. He'd finally got the security of a steady income and enough stability to let him focus even more on the creative process of writing new songs.

Meanwhile all the villagers were completely crazy about the minstrel and his music and they didn't mind digging deep in their purses to pay for it all. And they weren't only paying for the minstrel's fortnightly performance. His signed desert flints were selling like hot cakes too. But this was nothing compared to the amount the lute player and his wife were paying for the right to use the melodies. The village chief's daughter was sure now that she was just at the start of something bigger than anyone had imagined.

That was the precise moment the music industry was born. At least, that's how it could have been. But when I speak of 'the music industry', what am I actually talking about? And what does that industry look like?

The music industry is a pyramid and the artist is right at the top. By the term 'artist' I mean a band, producer, DJ or solo artist. Below the artist there's a whole food chain of individuals who help keep the pyramid as strong as possible. You can see the pyramid on page 19.

I'll now give you a brief introduction to the most influential elements of the pyramid.

The Artist
That's who it's all about. Without an artist, there'd be no pyramid.

The Manager
Below the artist you'll find the manager, the one who looks after the artist's interests.

These could just be their business interests, although there are plenty of managers who also take care of personal matters. Some artists have more than one manager or management agency. In such cases, you're usually talking about two managers: a general manager and someone for the business. The general manager keeps an eye on everything. The business

manager specializes in all the business aspects of the artistic life. But that role could also be fulfilled by someone else, a lawyer, for example. A lawyer is hired by the manager or directly by the artist. That means that the lawyer can keep tabs on the manager and vice versa.

The manager is like a spider in the centre of a web, guiding the whole team. That team includes the record company, producer, publisher, agent, and perhaps sponsors as well. Below this team, there's a whole range of other people ready for action, such as broadcasters, radio DJs, venues, and concert or festival promoters.

The Record Company

The record company – or label – is the part of the pyramid that makes sure the music gets an audience. So, if you've recorded a song, then the label makes sure it gets into the stores, or online equivalent. That started with singles and LPs, then cassette tapes and CDs, and now we're in the internet consumption era.

You should see the record label as the link between the artist, the fan, and the future fan. It's the label's job to ensure that as many people as possible are exposed to the artist and their music and in as many possible ways. In the past, record companies sometimes even wanted to 'create' artists themselves. That dates back to the time when companies had songwriters under contract and would search out the right artists for the songs. Modern examples are boybands and girl bands like Take That, Spice Girls, New Kids on The Block and Milli Vanilli. But The Supremes, The Monkees and even The Jacksons were also (partly) put together by their record companies. Nevertheless that role has changed over the years: producers and managers have now largely taken over the creative element.

That is one of the reasons why the number of functions in a record company is much smaller nowadays. The norm now is to hire a lot of external parties to carry out the work that used to belong to the label itself, for example the roles of music pluggers or agents. So to make it easier for you to see who's who, we'll look at three important elements inside a record company: A&R managers, product managers (sometimes known as 'brand managers') and promoters.

A&R managers mainly focus on the artistic development of an artist's career. 'A&R' stands for 'artist and repertoire' and obviously these managers make sure that the artist and their repertoire live up to their promise. They're the ones who shape the artist, in effect. What often happens is that choices have to be made from a whole range of producers and songwriters. In short: which song will the artist sing and what will it sound like? In other words, they'll decide how the artist can get the best song and the style it will have.

An example: Ed Sheeran has written a song with guitar accompaniment; he sings it by himself and records it. It's ready to send into the world. Or: Ed Sheeran has written a song, Bruno Mars wrote the chorus, and Chris Stapleton improved the lyrics. The recording has been enriched with orchestral backing and an extra rhythm section, and as well as Ed Sheeran singing and playing the guitar, there are vocals and guitar riffs from Bruno and Chris too.

Both versions could be huge hits. So, the A&R manager predicts – preferably before a single note is recorded – which would be the best version.

Product managers or *brand managers* are people whose main job is to promote the music delivered by the A&R manager and place it on the market. In theory, this is their only involvement with the music. They mainly focus on the artist's image and on answering the question: how can I get as much exposure for the artist as possible, so the public will buy the biggest possible amount of their music?

Promotional staff have the job of putting the product manager's strategies into action. They're the ones who make sure that the posters go up, that people talk about the artist online, and that there are interviews in all the right places. They also engage music pluggers to try to get the music played on radio stations and streaming services. But PR staff also develop ways of getting the artist more visibility on the radio, tv, online and in shops.

The Producer
The producer takes care of the way the artist sounds. In the past, the producer sat at the mixing desk and helped to find the artist's own sound.

Some important producers, past and present, are Quincy Jones (best known for his work with Michael Jackson), Butch Vig (the genius behind Nirvana's *Nevermind*) and George Martin (for ever associated with The Beatles).

As in the Ed Sheeran example, the producer works out (usually along with the artist) who will be part of the line-up, what instruments they'll play and how the track will be built up and structured. It's the producer, for example, who'll come up with the idea of using an orchestra. Sometimes the producer will also collaborate in the writing of a song, and sometimes they'll 'compile' it. That means that some elements of the song will be written by others and then put together in such a way that it becomes a whole. Someone writes a catchy refrain, someone else writes the lyrics, and yet another person creates the bass line and the melody. The producer will then search for a suitable voice and for other musicians, if necessary. This process lets them put together the best possible song.

Advances in technology mean that it's now a lot easier to produce music at home, making the music production profession much more accessible. After all, you can work much faster online and you've got a bigger range of options. Nowadays there are many more talented producers than in the past, and they all have their own style of production. That accessibility has made the role of the producer in contemporary music much more important and so you get to hear far more about them. That's mainly because a number of well-known DJs are also producers and because a number of well-known producers now choose to stand in the spotlight.

The Publisher
The publisher is responsible for managing the rights to the music. Whole books have been written on this topic, and as it's an incredibly complex and convoluted subject, I'm not going to explain it all in detail here. In fact, publishers like to keep things complex, so that no one will really understand how it works. But it comes down to this: if a song you've written, in part or alone, is played or performed, by you or someone else, you'll receive a payment for it. Such fees, or royalties, can be very lucrative, and as a consequence there are plenty of people who'd like to help artists with this source of income. Not only by collecting the fees, but also by exploiting the music in other ways. Think of films, games or

adverts, for example. As I've already said, this is a complex area with many opportunities that you'll only understand if a certain type of blood runs through your veins. This may all sound a bit vague, but publishers are vague too, and so I'll discuss this topic again in another chapter.

The Agent
The agent takes care of the live music element. There are usually two agents with responsibility for an artist's live shows worldwide. One focuses entirely on North America and is based in the US, and one is responsible for the rest of the world, and will usually be based in London. It's important to know that agents don't organize concerts. Agents sell the rights for putting on a show. They have a worldwide network and so can phone contacts for shows in every country. Agents are responsible for the tour planning, which means they work out how the artist can perform in the greatest number of countries in the shortest possible time. They must have good geographical knowledge and need to be familiar with the regulations of all the various countries. For example, you need to be aware of any border problems in Eastern Europe to work out how long it will take to drive from Berlin to Moscow. It's not unknown that a show can't go ahead because the band is stuck at the border, unwilling to pay a bribe to get through.

The Promoter
The contacts that agents have in every country are called promoters. Promoters buy the right to organize a show. They know exactly where in their country the artist will get the best chance to shine. They're aware of where and how they can get the best financial results, through good ticket price policies, for example. This means they can work out if they're able to offer enough money to get an artist to give a show in their region.

What's left isn't unimportant
I don't want to classify the remaining parties under the heading 'unimportant' because they all add immense value to the whole. In many cases, they're even indispensable. But you don't have to be a rocket scientist to know that a radio station plays songs, a music store sells CDs, and a festival or venue books the artist. Then T-shirts and other items portraying the artist are sold by the merchandiser, and the accountant makes sure that everything tallies.

And there you have it – a good overview of the pyramid. And now we can move across to the exceptions. Because it sometimes happens that the promoter is also the manager or that the producer is the artist as well. There are agents who own a concert hall and recording companies who also have a booking agency. But sponsors are always people who hand over money and want something from the artist in return. And merchandisers, as we saw, sell T-shirts printed with the band's logo. Although there are some merchandisers who also own agencies... and so it goes, on and on.

The Fan

Although fans aren't officially part of the industry, it's impossible to leave them out of the story. There are only two factors in the entire pyramid concept that are vital to the artist's survival, and apart from the artist, that's the fan. To keep things simple for the moment, we'll divide the fans into two categories: the superfan and the normal fan. The only real difference between them is their level of enthusiasm for the artist.

An example: Michael Jackson's final studio album was *Invincible*. The record label decided to release it with five different album covers so they could sell as many albums as possible. Apart from the colour, they were all identical. The true superfan bought all five albums. Normal fans simply bought their favourite colour. By the way, the promoter repeated the same trick for Jackson's London show, the one that was cancelled because of his death. The fans who'd bought a ticket for the show could get either a refund or an original printed version of the admission ticket, with a choice of no less than seven different designs.

The superfan will go through fire for their artist; they want absolutely everything to do with them and have to be at every show. The normal fan is quite simply just a little less fanatical. However, you can also include fellow travellers in the category of 'normal fan'. These are the people who just tag along with the real fans, but who'll still buy the album, the T-shirt or the printed oven glove at a concert. They're perhaps not the sort of fan who'll ask an artist for an autograph, but they definitely will tell their friends that they've discovered a great artist. And that's what an artist needs to have success and gain a large audience: ambassadors who'll tell their own network that an artist is really good. So then it makes sense to always keep an eye on the fans and take good care of them. Because if these ambassadors turn against the artist, their career will very likely crash.

The Unwritten Rule

So there you have it, more or less everything that makes up the pyramid. But I still have to explain its most important feature. If you're going to do business there, there's one unwritten rule: it works from the top to the bottom, and although it does sometimes work the other way round, from the bottom to the top, you must never break the food chain. In other words: you mustn't skip any of the steps. A promoter never makes deals with the manager and an agent doesn't phone the venue. It's as simple as that. To keep the whole industry intact, the pyramid must be preserved. Moreover, managers are usually very bad promoters, publishers are terrible agents, and record labels are really not that great at promoting bands. Not so long ago, promoters did venture into the business of releasing albums and record companies started organizing concerts. Spurred on by a desire for cross-pollination, the music industry spent a couple of years shouting that the future was in so-called 360 degree deals. That's why Madonna signed with Live Nation for all her activities, but in the end it was Universal who released the album. But more about that later.

Ultimately there's only one undeniable truth. The artist is at the top of the pyramid and the fans are at the bottom. Everything that happens in between is to make it seem that the artist is as close to those fans as possible. So the record company makes sure that the music reaches the fans. The agent makes sure that the artist sees the fans in real life, in a concert hall. The merchandiser and the retailer bring a little bit of the band closer to the fan. If you look at it like this, it's a strange model, because it really should be the other way round: the fan should be on top. If only because artists are completely crazy.

But if you're a manager you need quite a few faulty genes too.

MANAGERS ARE COMPLETELY CRAZY

It looks like a cushy number, being the manager of an artist or a band. You get flown all over the world, meet the most extraordinary people and you're always welcome everywhere you go. The most wonderful parties, the best restaurants, places that ordinary folk can only dream of. And you can – if only a little – set your stamp on the artist's career. And if you really go all out, perhaps you'll generate some form of fame for yourself too, and so get a taste of all the goodies that go with being an artist.

But it's much more down to earth than it seems. There are plenty of music management training courses, but it basically isn't possible to learn how to be a manager in advance. The vast majority of managers landed in the business by accident, because they happened to be in the artist's circle. Classic examples are being 'so-and-so's cousin', 'so-and-so's best friend', or – better still – 'so-and-so's mum or dad'. And that's not such a bad thing either, because managing an artist is more like being someone's coach or best friend than being a business partner.

Obviously a whole load of business decisions need to be made, but you can learn how to do that yourself, through trial and error. And of course, you'll let a specialist lawyer draw up important deals, such as record or publishing deals. With a bit of luck that specialist will also be able to do the negotiations. That costs a little money, but preserves your relationship with the other side. Don't forget that when all the deals have been made, the most difficult work of a manager is done. The dealmaking period is over. That's the period when the foundation is laid for the near future of the artist's career. And the foundation has to be good, because as the manager you only want to work with the best people and never have to switch again. But more about that later.

So, what's left then for a manager to do?

- The main job is to say no to all those fun ideas that happen to come by. By this I mean, partnerships or various entities who think your artist would be a perfect fit for their product or movement.

- Then you've got to give the record company the occasional telling-off because there hasn't been enough marketing for the album and the singles.

- And you give the agent or the promoters a kick up the pants because they haven't sold enough tickets.

- And give the agent or hospitality company a kick up the pants because they haven't sold enough VIP tickets.

- You chase up the merchandiser because they haven't sold enough merch.

- And chase up the publisher because big films or commercials aren't using enough of your artist's songs.

- And give the artist a kick up the pants because they really do have to write new hits (in other words: there has to be new music.)

I'm not going to claim that the above list means you've got nothing to do at all, but you don't need a really high level of education to give a few people a good kick up the pants. No, the biggest challenge is: how do you control your artist?

A common saying in the music industry is: 'We take care of things for the artists, so they can focus on the artistic process.' It's completely logical and understandable that artists who are given full rein for creative expression become less and less bothered about the chores that normal people don't enjoy doing. There are plenty of examples of artists who sit around like a sack of potatoes in all the necessary meetings during the dealmaking period. The most important job for the manager is to keep the artist sufficiently interested in the business side of things, but not so much that they start interfering.

And then the manager has to make sure that the artist spends as much time as possible on the creative process and, of course, on their image. After all, you really do want your artist to look something like the photos on their first album, so they're still recognizable. In other words: you have to act a little like a parent and nurture them. It's not much different with children: you've got to make sure they behave themselves a little (even when they're dealing with the big bad world) and that they learn something from what people say; but most of all, they've got to be allowed to be children. Parents know that there's really not much difference. And so it isn't strange that most managers are friends or family: you accept things from them that you wouldn't from others; they don't have a hidden agenda (if things are going well) and they always, unconditionally, have your best interests at heart. Add to that the fact that you're going to be around that person twenty-four hours a day, and the calculation is quickly completed: the manager is, or will become, someone who's already close to you. And mostly that isn't an outsider who just happens to have finished their music management degree at the very point you pick up the microphone. Most managers just fall into it: they didn't have that ambition from the start and began against their better judgment. And actually those are usually the best managers.

The managers who followed a course? They've gobbled up all the theory, they've hung on the words of more or less everyone in the industry, or they were once in a band themselves and got the idea they should go into management because they wanted to do something good for the industry. And they really do mean well, but still they're partly there by virtue of 'not quite having made it as an artist themselves'. Because being a manager really isn't fun. It's impossible to nurture artists who don't know what to do with their lives. Or to develop artists who don't take responsibility for anything, because others are already doing that for them. So, becoming a manager via a music management course isn't fun at all. Don't do it. But becoming a manager because you hang around a lot with your friends or family and you could earn your living from it: go ahead. Perhaps you'll even learn something from it.

And if you're smart and things are going well, you'll make it a lot easier for yourself by hiring a *day-to-day* manager. These are novice managers, who take on an artist's everyday chores. They're usually interns or people who have recently rolled into the job. Usually the drummer's best friend's cousin or brother. But the day-to-day manager is living proof that you really mustn't become a manager. After all, why do they exist? Not because being a manager is a really great profession, because the day-to-day manager has to deal with all the dirty jobs. The real manager doesn't feel like doing them anymore, because after a few months they're already sick and tired of keeping that unguided missile under control. Day-to-day managers are also known in the industry as 'babysitters'. They're the ones who have to charge to the rescue if an insect flies into the artist's hotel room. They've got to pay the bills for smashed-up gear and do everything the managers themselves don't like doing. With a bit of luck the day-to-day manager will have a tour manager for the live shows, because then some of those chores can be passed a bit further down the line. But at some point there's no more cake to delegate out.

No wonder then that artist managers are always happy with local record companies, festivals and radio stations. They always have people on hand to pamper the artist: so-called artist handlers, who take care of everything that the artist (or the tour manager) demands. It's like a game to them, answering positively to as many questions as possible and being as swift as possible in delivering everything requested. Then the artist is happy and the manager too.

You can ask yourself why managers ever begin this job at all. As I've already said, most of them simply fall into the work by chance, but it's also lucrative. As the manager, you're almost at the top of the pyramid, which also means that you're exactly where the money is shared out. Your place is directly below the artist, so in theory they don't need to share with anyone other than the manager. And then there's all the other kind of income, from merchandise, live shows, sponsorship, album revenue, and publishing. You may not be in it for the money, but once you get a little success the cash does start coming in. The only question is: which way will the pennies roll?

WHO GETS WHAT PIECE OF THE PIE?

'Sharing the profits never made anyone poorer.' This wise saying is often forgotten, because it's a difficult one for accountants and money-conscious entrepreneurs to understand. And indeed, when everyone's getting hot under the collar about everything that could possibly be earned, people often forget that if you can't share, you can't grow – however much of a cliché that may sound. So let's take a proper look at what gets shared out in the music world. You'll have to use your imagination for this, because we're going to visit a patisserie. For the sake of convenience, I'll present all the revenue derived from musical endeavours as a delicious apple pie.

Let's look at the base of the pie, the record deals. The amount shared out from that is usually between 10 and 25 percent. That's for the artist! I'm talking about so-called 'artist deals', in which the record label bears all the costs and the artist, in theory, doesn't run any risks. One of those risks, for example, could be having to pay back an advance. With an artist deal the record label doesn't only take on all the risks, but pays all the costs relating to the recordings. If the artist pays the recording costs themselves, then you're talking about a licensing deal, in which the record company will bear the costs (and risks) of promotion and distribution. Or you're talking about a distribution deal, in which the artist takes responsibility for everything, except the distribution of the albums (both physical and digital). In that case, it's the record company that gets between 10 and 20 percent, although then they're usually called the distributor.

The pie's filling comes from the publishers. They ask for a third of the entire copyright. That means: all the revenue from playing and performing the songs written by the artist. But they do everything that's necessary to generate and manage that income, such as the administration, setting up song-writing camps, and linking the artist up with co-writers.

So, now we have the pie crust and the filling, but what about the whipped cream?

That comes from the live shows. Agents usually receive between 10 and 15 percent of the guaranteed fees. As long as the shows go through, they're bound to get that income. Concert organizers (promoters) get 15 percent, on average. They generally have to guarantee a fixed sum on top of that to secure the tour, so that the artist is assured of a basic income. Once that guarantee and the production costs have been covered, that's when the promoter's slice of the pie kicks in.

There are other sources of income too, which may be somewhat less important, but can certainly boost the coffers. Income from merchandise and sponsoring, for example. At any rate, these forms of income have become more and more important over the past few years. Let's call them the cherry on the top.

And now we have a lovely pie filled with lots of delicious fruit, and various people have already got the promise of a nice percentage. Let's share it out. The manager usually gets between 15 and 25 percent, but the question is: where does that percentage come from? That varies quite a bit. The agreement could be that their share is based on all the artist's revenues. In that case, everything that comes in is the basis of the payment. So, a slice of the whole pie. But another common way of doing this is that the manager gets a percentage of all the income, apart from the copyright revenues (which include the income from performance licences). In that case you're dividing the pie without its apple filling. One of the reasons for this is that inexperienced managers sometimes forget to specify copyright revenues in the deal. Another, perhaps more plausible reason, is that you don't include the creation of the songs in the deal, or their rights and any direct income from them. In that case, you could argue that the manager has had very little influence on the songs as such, while, of course, they've generated a huge amount of added value when making the exploitation deals for the songs.

The rest of the pie goes to the artist, unless they've opted for a deal in which all the revenue goes into one pot and there's a fifty-fifty or three-thirds share-out. In that case the artist, the record label and the artist's manager are the parties involved. These may potentially be supplemented by promoters or investment companies. How this kind of deal is struck very much depends on where you are in your career as an artist. In practice, it's usually the bigger artists, with excellent accountants, who are sometimes tempted by this model. It looks a bit like a 360 degree deal, but in this case the artist is also one of the parties.

All the numbers I've mentioned look like nice percentages, but in rock 'n' roll it's completely normal practice that no two deals are the same. So don't assume that all deals will follow the above pattern, but expect the most exhaustive and varied deals imaginable. All the available options, such as bulk discounts, kickbacks, and bonuses, are eagerly used: 'You'll get a share of the kickback'; 'You'll get a bonus if the festival sells out'; or 'Your percentage will increase on an annual basis.'

What's more interesting, however, is the idea behind the industry's self-proclaimed equality principle. Something you'll often find in a contract, as part of the deal, is the Most Favoured Nations clause. In other words: if another artist ends up earning more than you or has got a better deal, then your deal is retroactively adapted to theirs. That's why there are artists who literally have clauses in their contracts stating that they must be the only act at the festival that gets the highest fee. And that no artist in the previous history of the festival should ever have received a higher fee. That kind of clause gave the financial department of a famous Dutch festival a very big surprise when they had to pay out a sum of 206,000 euros. Sure enough: exactly 1,000 euros more than the headliner had been paid the previous year. Fortunately, that kind of clause doesn't apply retroactively to all the acts who played before, although you never can tell what kinds of deals will be dreamt up in the future.

YOU DON'T SEE THE BIGGEST EARNERS

Parties, festivals, conferences and shows. That's where you really get to know each other. True, you can fly around the world for group gatherings, and meet with other people till you drop. But at the end of the day the best way to get to know people in the industry is to go to plenty of places where they 'all hang out'. And then you're talking about parties, festivals, conferences and shows.

But shows are actually the worst place for networking. The booker, promoter, agent and manager are always tied up with the show. The record label people are nervously hanging around till the point when they can present the gold record. That's usually scheduled for before the performance, but to keep the guests and employees of the record company in the house a bit longer, most managers end up postponing it till after the show.

Parties are definitely a good place to begin building up your network, but try getting an invitation! Album launches are parties in one sense, but to be completely honest the only people you're likely to meet are a couple of promoters for local bars and some journalists who haven't been allowed to speak to the artist but still want to send in some copy. Let's look at an example: one of Lily Allen's album launches was held under a bridge in London. Painted fridges, street artists busy doing their regular thing all around us and ultracool DJs doing their stuff from the top of car wrecks. Fantastic setting, just a shame that Lily herself wasn't there. The launch party had been scheduled to happen right after the launch show, so she was tired. No Team Allen then. So who was there? The press hounds and record company guests, the hired musicians and their hangers-on, and even a handful of Lily's own fans were all at that 'legendary' party. As for the 'important people', naturally, they were nowhere to be seen.

Festivals are a good place for networking, but then you need the right kind of wristband. It won't work with an ordinary wristband - that only gets you onto the festival ground and that's the last place the music industry's important people want to show themselves. And a service pass won't open many doors either. Service passes are wristbands that show you're working as part of the catering or festival cleaning teams, for example. If you're doing that kind of work, then it's hard to join in the conversations (although you'd be surprised at how many people in the industry did – once upon a time – start behind the festival bar. That's just a tip!)

And now the next door: if you've got a Press or Guest wristband, then you're heading in the right direction. That lets you into the special Press/Guest area and that's definitely where it happens! Although everyone will agree that this kind of wristband is mainly useful because of the clean washrooms (which aren't too bad even at the end of the evening). But to be fair, the Press/Guest area really is quite holy ground. That's because the invitation policy at every festival is based on the following theory. You've got to let journalists in because they're promoting your festival, so they need somewhere they can quietly write their reviews and send them through, or a place where they can edit their photos. Then you've got the festival organizer's guests, and what do you do with them? Are you going to let them loose on the festival grounds or let them go backstage with the artists? But if you let them go there, they'll only get in the way. And more importantly, you don't want tipsy girlfriends or mothers-in-law mingling with the artists, because that's something the artists really don't need. So that's where the following idea has come from: we'll make a place between the festival site and the backstage area, put a bar there and a couple of posh porcelain toilets, call it the Press/Guest Area, and the problem's solved. An added benefit is that you've then got a place where you – as a music industry bigwig – can have a quick chat with people without having to drag them backstage. The ideal place, then, to meet like-minded people and occasionally tug at the sleeve of a stray industry guru.

I'll spare you the details of the rest of the wristband collection, such as 'VIP', 'Staff Camp', bike wristbands (yes, truly) or the shadowy world of travel passes, hologram stickers and colour-coded lanyards. The ultimate in wristbands is quite simply the backstage wristband, also called the 'AAA-wristband' (AAA stands for 'Access All Areas'). Every festival has its own naming system, but what I'm talking about here is the wristband that lets you into the dressing rooms and all other relevant places. Of course, you've also got AAAA-wristbands ('All Authorities, All Access') or AAAAA-wristbands ('Access All Areas, All Authority'). These give you access to, for example, the festival's strongbox or the landowner's cycle shelter.

Back to the backstage wristband, because that lets you into the dressing room area and that's where the tour managers, managers, promoters and product managers are. That's the place to see and be seen because once in a blue moon an industry bigwig may drop by. You know, the gamechangers and the gurus.

Otherwise you'll only see them very occasionally at conferences. Usually because they're part of a panel discussion or they're meeting up with someone who is on a panel. They're a bit harder to spot at night, because they tend to dine in restaurants where ordinary people aren't allowed. So target the daytime and backstage at festivals, or go to conferences. Day conferences are useful anyway, because in a short period of time you can acquire a wealth of information just by going to a few panels. That said, you need to realize that the real information will never be mentioned out loud. If the discussion is about the illustrious world of ticket resales, for example, then everyone in the panel will say it's disgraceful, or not, but no one will tell you in any kind of detail how much profit ticket resales make. And that's precisely what we all want to know.

So conferences and backstage at festivals are the places to be and where you have to create something of an impression. Preferably a good one. The top manager who stood on a table during a dinner party, and then dropped his trousers, hasn't been active in the music industry for some time now. The agent who fled into the city in the middle of the night without his phone because he was scared of being murdered by a bipolar goth girl is also not very happy that the story leaked out. Although you have to realize that these kinds of stories can also contribute to someone's cult status. Two local promoters were once meant to be chairing a panel after an all-nighter, with all the alcohol that implies. What followed was a discussion full of shouting and swearing, which ended with fisticuffs and panellists walking out. Not chic, perhaps, but rather impressive. And years later, in spite of what happened, one of those promoters is still firmly in the saddle.

Now that we've established where you should be and how not to make an impression, the big question is: is that it then? No. It's true that these are great places to be and that you can all have lots of fun there, messing around in the margins, and with a good or even fantastic salary – but the real work? The real work happens away from the parties, festivals, shows and conferences. The really big sacks of money are brought into places you'll never see.

What about where publishers hang out, for example? They don't need the kind of network you find at festivals. What they need are songwriters and artists, and they've got to get them on board before the shows and festivals start. Publishers are silent forces in the music industry, who rake in the money without ever needing to be visible. The only time you'll ever see them together is at the annual awards for the Song of the Year or the Best Multi-songwriter Song. Not entirely coincidentally there'll be a red carpet, a four course dinner, and everyone will be wearing evening clothes. You'll see songwriters there too, big earners if they've got a few hits to their name. Producers and record company executives: plenty of those at these dinner parties for the big money-makers.

Who will pick up the bill for the evening? That's right: the Music Publishers Association and the music rights representatives. In other words, this branch of the business is so well-organized that they can get away with cutting artists' earnings for the award ceremonies. A ceremony where you basically rip yourself off so you can stick feathers in your friends' and colleagues' caps. There are ceremonies like this every month across the world, and some of them even need the artist's presence (and performance) to sell the broadcasting rights. It's no big secret that artists get hefty fees to show their faces at this kind of event. The longer the list of artists, the more licence revenue can be generated. And in any case the artist usually bags some kind of prize. And it's no big secret either that the most impressive parties are given by one and the same organization and that the same artists show up every year. Dick Clark Productions is behind the American Music Awards, the Golden Globe Awards and the Billboard Music Awards, for example. Plenty of food there for conspiracy theories. But all in all, not a bad business model. And that sort of thing keeps it all nicely going.

Let's return for a moment to the invisible big-money earners. The real deals, done by the big bosses, are made on the proverbial golf course. That's a cliché, of course, and an idea that might seem out of date. But it's not such a crazy idea to work out how many people at the top of the industry literally do strike a ball. Not so long ago I started playing the noble sport myself, and I can tell you, a whole world opens up for you. But if it's not golf, then it's some other kind of sport or place where it's not easy to get admitted. In any case, most of the major deals are still made at the periphery of the industry, so not in the most beautiful meeting room at the office. And that's how it should be too, because the best and most extraordinary deals are not usually made in a place where everyone feels at ease. The art of making a deal doesn't lie in being able to negotiate well. It boils down to creating positive conditions which can get you a good deal. And that doesn't happen backstage, because nothing exciting happens there at all, I can tell you.

BACKSTAGE ETIQUETTE

When the Head of Security for Oasis tried to explain for the third time that I wasn't supposed to use the dressing room door as a football goal, it finally sunk in. And when the lads from indie rock band The View drove a stolen golf buggy into a ditch, that was the end of that story too. Because what seems enormously exciting from the outside, turns out to be a real disappointment behind the scenes.

Backstage: the place where it all happens. Where the lads become men and the girls become women. Where you're bombarded with sex, drugs and rock 'n' roll. Where without realizing it, and far too eagerly, you step across your own boundaries.

Most of the backstage area of a festival actually looks like a container camp, with production people rushing around like crazy. With a bit of luck they'll have put up some streamers or other decoration. The artists are usually in their bus, giving interviews, or they're in the dressing room. And if they sometimes come outside to play together, all they do is chat to each other. No, getting access backstage at a festival is mainly handy because the toilets are cleaned more regularly than on the site and there's somewhere to keep dry when it rains.

Let's take a step or two back in time. The term 'backstage' comes from the world of film and theatre. The backstage area was mainly seen as the place where people were busy with casting, make-up and costumes. The place where the business was done that you didn't see on stage, where the offices were, where the actors changed their costumes, the camera crew ate their sandwiches, and the rest of the crew and cast had a smoke. The place where the changing rooms were. But it was also where auditions were held, for example, and all the business deals were made. The fact that every reputable entertainment company nowadays has gigantic offices in city centres simply means that business no longer happens behind the stage.

The backstage area has become a place where people wait and prepare for that one moment: being on stage. Then after an hour and half of fireworks, they go backstage again. And it's an understatement to say that such places are absolutely vital. You really need somewhere comfortable where you can get ready, although you can sometimes end up in some kind of cubbyhole. Because the proverbial broom cupboard often turns out to be not really that proverbial. There are still plenty of places where there's no backstage at all and you have to get changed in the utility room or in the little room next door. Not exactly the stuff of legend.

It may seem a little exaggerated to say that the term 'backstage' has taken on legendary proportions, but things certainly do happen there that should never go near the stage. Because, however authentic and realistic it may seem, the stage is the place of illusion. Real reality is what we see all around us, all day long, each and every day.

But the place behind the illusion has its own rules of etiquette that everyone should obey, whether it's the backstage of a theatre, a festival or concert hall. You mustn't behave like a groupie, for example, unless, of course, you are one. But even then it's best not to emphasize that too much. Besides, artists can see from a mile away whether you're there for the music or something more carnal, so don't worry about choosing how to act. No groupie behaviour, and nothing related to it either, i.e. fan behaviour. Fan behaviour can best be described as the kind that makes you head straight for the artists, preferably running and screaming, with the sole aim of meeting your favourite artist in person. That's absolutely not allowed backstage, because the whole idea of the backstage area is that there are no fans there. Unless they've been specially invited, but then there's previous warning (and it's been paid for in advance). So if you're the fan of a specific artist and you want to meet them in person, the best thing is to be as professional as possible and slowly edge your way towards them.

I once approached Dave Grohl like that, very professionally of course, but he saw me coming, so just before the supreme moment I veered off to the right and introduced myself to his agent. Possibly the most childish thing I've ever done. Though I have to admit that encouraging an agent to use a shower as a lavatory isn't a trophy I proudly display in my cabinet either. So, a better example might be the publisher who tried to get an artist to sign a deal backstage. After saying his piece, he asked the artist in question to autograph a CD for him. That was quite enough for the artist and the publisher lost the deal of his life. He has got a signed CD of Adele on his shelves, though – and I have never yet managed to shake Dave Grohl's hand.

In any case, behaving like a groupie, fan, or little kid is not the sort of thing that scores you points backstage. Moreover, the most important thing is to get in the tour manager's, production manager's or artist's way as little as possible. Because backstage it's the tour manager who is basically in charge. They're paid to make things run as smoothly as possible and they don't want to deal with anything disruptive. That's why the tour manager always sighs when the record company comes and hands over yet another Gold Record. Not only does that waste a lot of time, but the artist never takes those things on tour with them, so why give them at all? Ah yes! For the photo opportunity, of course.

So you've got to stay friends with the tour manager, and with the production manager too. The production manager is the one who makes the show run well, so if you want to stand in the wings, or at the mixing desk, or right in the middle of the auditorium, you've got to get into their good books. And of course you need to be aware of where the crucial flexes and cables are, because accidentally kicking a plug out somewhere is a disaster for the show and for your relationship with the crew.

The artist's tour and production managers actually listen to just one person, and that's the venue's production manager (okay, very occasionally they listen to the promoter as well). That's because the venue production manager has to do all the odd jobs, such as consulting with the venue security and making sure there are enough towels. These three people make up the team that ensures that the show will go on, to perfection. All the other people – with the exception of the artist, of course – only create noise, and that's not what you want at all. And this, more or less, is the basic principle of those unwritten backstage rules.

You're probably wondering who else you'll find behind the scenes. Well, there's the artist's crew, local crew, band members' partners, band members' friends, record company people, friends of the promoter, the promoter themself, friends of the crew, publishers, managers, the publishers' friends, various managers' business acquaintances, sponsors, the sponsors' friends, stagehands, runners, doctors, washers-up, people who work in catering, bus drivers, security personnel, friends of the security personnel, friends of the tour manager and the production manager, other artists who have just dropped in to say hi, other tour managers who want to see what's going on, production managers who've come to take a look at the production, the band's lawyers and tour accountants – just to mention a few. In short: you'll mostly find people backstage who actually have no business to be there, but who all firmly believe that's where they ought to be.

But are all those preconceptions about sex, drugs and rock 'n' roll a big lie then? Okay, I'll admit it, I once had to stand around waiting with ten other people for the bassist of a band because he wanted to show a girlfriend his 'new car'. Well, we were waiting for the band to leave for their private jet and fly off to their next show, so there wasn't really much chance that we'd believe he had his car with him. But to be honest, you see more people in tears because the artists didn't give them any special attention than people who did. Yes, the washrooms are sometimes visited by several people at the same time, although things have got a lot more innocent in recent years. So I've been told. The only time I had to face one of my greatest fears was when two managers invited me to join them for a few lines of cocaine. I mustered up all the courage I could and said: 'Sorry, no thanks'. But when they answered drily, 'Great, then there'll be more for us', the fear that I might lose business connections by turning down such things completely vanished.

There are a number of important rules of backstage etiquette.

1. The first is to do with drink, although this rule is regularly forgotten, not least because of drinking. The rule is clear: never drink the artist's fridge dry. You may laugh at this, but it's one of the commonest problems that a tour manager really doesn't want to deal with. The reason is this: organizers generally don't put enough drinks in the dressing rooms, because they know people will always ask for more. And nine times out of ten those drinks will be consumed either before or during the show, when the band isn't drinking all that much or they're already on stage. Nothing's worse than a thirsty artist coming offstage and not being able to open a can of beer (or something

stronger) because their entourage has already guzzled the lot. So don't do it and make sure it doesn't happen.

2. The second rule is something that people backstage sometimes forget. Give the artist some time before bursting in. Give them at least fifteen minutes before and fifteen minutes after the show to get ready, get their breath back, change their clothes, or evaluate their performance before you knock on the door.

3. And here follows the next tip: always knock on the door before you enter. That will save a lot of embarrassing moments, although you'd probably have plenty of good stories to tell.

4. Then there's the question of how to interact with the artists backstage. You could make a whole sub-category of that in terms of manners. One of the most important things to remember is that you should never bring bad news before the start of a show. And not after the show either, in fact. Bad news or bad jokes before the show can ruin the whole performance. Once, when I was still a venue promoter, I had to explain to the electronic pop group Elevator Suite that I couldn't find their potential drug supplier's number. After what I think was the worst show of their (brief) career, the band members rushed off the stage, through the audience, towards their tour manager. The very same tour manager who assured them he'd now got hold of the 'pharmacist's' contact details. So no silly jokes beforehand.

5. As well as never bringing bad news, it's best not to have any kind of business meeting before the artist goes on stage. First of all, you've got a deadline – at some point the artist will have to get ready for the performance. And that's something they can do whenever it suits them. So if there are difficult issues, the conversation will simply be cut off. Secondly – although I'm not a neuroscientist, of course – the artist has to use a specific half of the brain to solve business problems. And they need exactly the other half to perform. Switching from one to the other apparently takes too much time, which means there's no more focus when the artist is onstage. And the result is nearly always a bad show. So never discuss business matters before a performance. Festivals are an exception to this: if the artist is playing early on in the day, there'll be plenty of time to go over things when the show is over.

But give yourself a good margin after the show, to let the adrenaline subside.

6. Then there's the most important question an artist can ask you backstage, the question everyone behind the scenes will have to deal with one day. What should you say when the artist asks you what you thought about the show? In all positive cases you should honestly tell them that it was fantastic, in every respect. The sound was good, it looked great, the audience were really into it, the lighting was perfectly timed and the build-up of the setlist was outstanding. But what if you've got some criticisms? Then you beat about the bush for the first hour and after that make sure you're gone. But you've got to give yourself some good training in beating about the bush without it being too obvious. A good tactic, for example, is to switch roles. So answer with: 'Yeah, it was great, wasn't it? Couldn't you feel that from the audience?' If the show itself was just not very good (someone did bring bad news again), you can always answer with: 'Wow! The sound and lighting were awesome!' At the point when you really can't get out of it, because the show was undeniably bad, you can open up a can of well-used (yet worthless) arguments. These are arguments with relevant (local) information that no one could have foreseen in advance. 'The room was a bit tame, maybe, but it's always like that in this area.' Or: 'The audience round here always talks during the songs. It wasn't actually all that bad.' Or otherwise you can always make an excuse: 'The meal didn't agree with me, I guess, because I was in the washroom and didn't see half of the show.' That's a common excuse, by the way, because after the opening song you were probably sitting in the bar next door already.

THE GATEKEEPERS

Everyone, from artist to music industry professional, has an equal chance of making it in the music world. But that idea is actually very naïve and unconvincing, and it makes no sense at all to think it's true. That's because it's patently obvious that the music industry depends on a system of who knows who, even though that topic is more hotly debated than ever. Inequalities are actually unavoidable, and it's inevitable that the system will sometimes be misused.

The most notorious examples are pressurizing, abusing or blackmailing artists in exchange for the promise of a glittering career. Then they really have to keep their wits about them to make a good decision: 'I can be what I always wanted, and here's my chance. But I'll have to do things in exchange that really aren't acceptable.' I can imagine how terrible such dilemmas are. Monstrous, even. But I can't do anything other than imagine them, because I have never consciously come across such situations. Although, looking back at things, there may well have been certain moments and decisions which perhaps wouldn't tick all the boxes nowadays, but as far as I'm concerned, I've always acted according to my conscience.

There's an area of tension here that is difficult to explain. Because it's also about mutual perceptions within the industry and the extent to which people are aware of each other's activities. I'm pretty sure, for example, that I've undervalued certain roles in this book, or that I'm explaining them differently. You can expect the general public not to understand how things work, but surely you can expect your colleagues to be up to date with all the ins and outs of the music industry?

I did once say in an interview, for example, that I thought it was ridiculous to have a female quota when booking festival acts. Immediately the whole feminist movement jumped on me – at least, just the feminist movement interested in music, so in the end it wasn't too bad at all. The biggest criticism was that as a festival you should set an example, because that's how you can influence the way your audience thinks. There is a grain of truth in that, but I would venture to suggest that it's just a small grain and one mainly based on a major misunderstanding that critics, (festival) promoters, radio stations, record companies and the media all seem to have.

The misunderstanding is that people perceive compilers as makers. And the compilers generally see themselves as makers too, which makes it even sadder. That's why festival promoters prefer to call themselves 'Artistic Directors', or something similar. But the difference between a programmer and an artist is huge. An artist is someone who makes something, who creates something out of nothing. A promoter is someone who chooses from things that are already made and makes a nice mixture from them. That mix is not at the same level as an artistic creation. A promoter, or artistic director, can be compared to someone who makes a mixtape, a cassette with the coolest songs of the time. That's all. And yet the idea exists that promoters have influence, or at the very least can exert it. That's a relic from the distant past, when record label executives could still tell the artist how to sing a song they themselves hadn't chosen. When promoters still had their say in the setlist and so could decide on the length of the performance. For the sake of convenience, let's call the people who still cling to these ideas 'gatekeepers'. In the past it was mainly old, white men who held such old-fashioned ideas. And yes, they do still exist, although thankfully they seem to be slowly vanishing.

We know that artists are the actual makers and we've already established that artists are the ones with influence. Why do the mere compilers of the music industry keep thinking that they're the gatekeepers? Festival programmes are indeed put together by promoters or artistic directors. After all, they're the ones who book the artists. But in the end, it's the artists who tell the story, not the combination of artists. It's normally the artists who'll get the tickets sold, and it's the artists who make the festival a success, or not. At least, I've never yet heard of a hugely successful festival with terrible acts that no one wants to see. I will admit that a festival can offer smaller acts a stage, which can give their career an extra boost. And that's one way in which you can play the role of gatekeeper a little. But you won't change the world like that, nor the opinions that exist in it. That's best left to the makers: the artists.

Yet the biggest misconception of the general public and the media is assigning huge amounts of influence to festival organizers, promoters and record companies. If you're looking for change, that's something you have to bear in mind. No, write it on your arm with a big fat marker pen.

Another example of overrating someone's influence: ticket prices. They're always too high and it's always the promoter's fault. That makes sense: 'after all they've got the contract with the artist and they can decide how much a ticket costs and how much VIP stuff they have to do'. That is the general public's opinion, but they've absolutely got the wrong end of the stick. If Lady Gaga's tickets go for $100, for example, then Ed Sheeran will price his tickets at $90 and Beyoncé at $125. Because Ed Sheeran will want to say that his tickets are cheaper than Lady Gaga's. And Beyoncé thinks she's a much bigger artist than Lady Gaga, and that's why you've got to ask more for her tickets.

In general, however, promoters try to keep the ticket prices as low as possible, because the risks are then much lower. And what about the VIP prices? They're worked out in exactly the same way as the ordinary tickets, but they're usually sold directly by the artist's VIP company, so without any involvement from the promoter. More and more, it's the artist who decides, together with the agent and the manager, roughly what the promoter should ask for the ticket. There you have it then: the promoter's influence on ticket prices is much smaller than you'd think.

Does the music industry do anything about this misconception? Not really. It's a pretty comfortable position too. Because who would voluntarily give away their imaginary power bubble?

METHUSELAH

Methuselah is the oldest living tree in the world: it germinated around 4,853 years ago, in the year 2832 BCE. But Methuselah's exact location is kept absolutely secret to protect it from vandalism. Well, I don't want to stretch the comparison too much, but many a music mogul still types with two fingers. And there are agents who, in spite of the invention of spreadsheets, still use paper and pencil to work out tour bookings. The music industry is as flexible as an old tree, yet there is still room for innovation. The rise of the internet, for example, has pushed the music industry into extreme progress. Everyone nowadays knows where the fans are, how best to reach them and how to squeeze the most money out of them, and that's owing to the digital world.

At the end of the nineties there was a shift from the physical world of music channels, discotheques and record stores towards the internet, and the field of play altered. You need to understand that releasing a song was still a rather expensive business up to then. Before any single even saw the outside world it had to be recorded, designed, pressed and packed. Then the single had to be sent to the dance floor, radio and record store. And, of course, a video clip had to be made for MTV or other music channels. So, whereas in the past the music industry had to physically bring the music to its audience, once the internet arrived potential artists had a platform to launch their music into the world themselves. Before they'd even got a design for the record sleeve.

It started with Myspace, where people could listen to music for free and have some real contact with the artist. That now seems very normal, but it was only possible in the past if you camped out in front of the star's hotel or became a member of their fan club. From the time that Myspace started, artists could have direct contact with their fans as well, making it much easier to build up a fanbase. Before any record label, agent or publisher had even heard of the artist. This change has meant that the majority of artists are no longer made by the industry – it's just allowed to piggyback on the artist's success. And if you don't want to join in with that, there are a hundred other candidates standing in the queue. What this means is that in recent years the artist has become far more important and influential.

You can find plenty of innovation in other areas too. Music used to be released on vinyl, then on cassettes. Then came the CD, and after that we were all downloading, and now we stream music. That makes it sound as if the music industry is incredibly radical and innovative, but these innovations didn't come from the music industry itself. Technological changes are eventually embraced by the music industry, but no one in a record company ever said: 'Now we've got the LP, maybe we should develop something digital.' On the contrary, the industry has fiercely resisted every form of change. Because you can copy tapes, you can endlessly burn music onto CDs, and you can easily share downloads with other people. And that isn't what all that wonderful music was meant for. Innovations in the music industry have always come from tech companies and not from music businesses. For example, Apple iTunes came to the rescue during the download era, and now Spotify is the company ensuring that music streaming generates revenue. Years earlier, it was Philips, the light bulb manufacturer, that invented the cassette tape and then the CD. If we dive even deeper into history, none of the inventors of the gramophone record – Léon Scott, Thomas Edison and Emile Berliner – worked for a music company.

Let's be clear then, the biggest changes in the music industry in terms of innovation have come more from companies with other areas of interest than from the music industry itself. Because in the past seventy years not much else has changed. Sure, the shows are a bit snazzier, and we now pay in tokens instead of with real money. The deals are sharper too, and the live industry is working like crazy on dynamic pricing, like you get in the travel industry. But when you compare today's music industry to the early days, there really aren't any huge differences at all. At eight o'clock the curtains still open for an hour and a half of magic, exactly as they did back then.

But that artists want to keep things under their own control and do more and more themselves is something you could definitely call a big change. And it's a logical development that artists' trust in some elements of the music industry has diminished and that they want to keep things in their own hands. When The Cure discovered that the company charging them thousands per hour for renting sound equipment was actually the band manager's company, they'd soon had enough of external parties. In such cases it's better to manage things yourself, as any blindfolded accountant can confirm.

No, the point I'm making is that the pyramid and its inhabitants are just as solid and steadfast as Methuselah, and certain laws go along with that. And they're not something you can swiftly change.

PART 2

THE ARTIST

An artist is someone who draws on their creative talents to make art and uses their gifts to perform in public.

What kinds of artists are there? What do they do? Where do they stand in the industry? How do people perceive them and how should you deal with them?

FROM NARCISSIST TO SUPERSTAR

This may sound a little strange, but an artist's appeal has nothing to do with the fact that they're really good at something. It's mainly to do with them being completely crazy, in both a positive and negative sense. What's more, most artists are very good at hiding this craziness. Musicians are usually very good actors too, and they have to be. It helps them to hide their inner craziness. That craziness comes in various forms, which I've labelled with some convenient terms to make things simpler.

1. The narcissist

Also known as the 'complete and utter egomaniac', the kind of artist who only thinks about themself.

These artists come into the business with a very high opinion of themselves. After all, they're prodigies and everyone's meant to idolize them. They're generally very introverted, only have a limited number of 'real' friends (in attendance as their professional entourage), splash their money around, and think status is more important than a long-term career. The industry treats them with care and caution, doing all it can to please them, however crazy. There's usually an extra assistant manager around to help out – a day-to-day manager – who hasn't been in the business that long, is still as green as grass, and finds everything exciting and a challenge.

This type of artist is usually a one-hit wonder and in the end the biz only puts up with them because they make money. That doesn't mean to say, of course, that these artists don't last more than a single hit. With a bit of luck, they'll have built up something of a live reputation, though they're bound to screw that up later by behaving badly in clubs or festivals. In other words, once the ticket sales for these artists start dropping, promoters would rather see the back of them.

Although these artists have no understanding of the industry at all, at some point they want to have a go at the business side of their career themselves. That makes sense to them, because in the end their failing career is everyone's fault but their own. Artists like that think: why am I paying such a high percentage for a disappointing result? And the new tour isn't selling well and the timing is completely wrong, so let's get rid of the agent because 'we haven't clicked for some time now, anyway.' Then a completely new team is brought in that tries everything all over again, with limited success, after which the artist sinks into oblivion. In some cases the musician still manages to get by with a bit of production work or some other little job in the industry. Usually, however, the candle gradually dies out and you never hear anything more of them again. Drink and drugs also play a major role in these lives, by the way, which after that short-lived career only makes things sadder. No, what's even sadder is that after a few years these artists always try to give it another go. I'd like to give you some examples of renewed success, but I really can't think of any.

2. The control freak
The artist who wants to keep everything, yes, everything, in their own hands.

Control freaks may have the urge for control in their DNA, but it's usually the product of having been cheated in the past. And to be fair, I have to say that there's nothing at all wrong with wanting control, to a certain extent. I've always advised the bands and artists I've dealt with in the past to do as much themselves as possible. And that's mainly because you can then keep an eye on how things are going, if only at a global level. It's really not a bad idea to understand what publishing is, how the tour finances work and the basic principles of a record deal. I even think this is essential for being a successful artist. But the control freak keeps hold of the reins because they don't trust their managers. Control freaks are always trying to reinvent the wheel, while the professionals around them nod sheepishly at brilliant ideas like: 'So let's let the fans decide what they want to pay per stream.' Just like narcissists, control freaks can initially get away with their behaviour, but in most cases being a know-all isn't a good basis for cooperation. You'll swiftly find that managers drop out (after all, the artist always knows better), record labels distance themselves (after all they've been saying for a long time that it wasn't a good single) and agents and promoters run away screaming (because according to the artist not enough posters were put up and the Facebook posts should have had better regional coverage).

You can spot these artists from the fact that they start out by holding discussions with all the other parties. And that they want another discussion after the first discussion. And that they then announce that they haven't yet chosen who they want to sign with. And that they follow this by holding as many meetings as possible about all the other elements of the business. Then they wonder why people have their own opinions and what's wrong with the suggested plans. And then they'll only sign when you do exactly what the control freak wants. Which isn't even necessary anymore, because the artist has already done most of it anyway.

Now, I don't think it's very polite to give examples of artists I've worked with who have such narcissistic tendencies. On the other hand, I wonder if they'd actually notice. I once took the initiative to stop the bookings for a particular artist. The response, after two months without any contact, was that I was informed that they'd unfortunately decided to end our partnership. I felt like I was back at school again.

3. The thinker
The artist who contributes plenty of ideas, but lets others do the work.

These are the nicest. They're not dumb, they secretly know exactly how things work, they listen to the advice of people in the music industry and as a result they're very popular. They're genuinely interested in all the ins and outs of the music world, but try to stay out of the firing range themselves. That's actually a good tactic: that means they're never perceived as the annoying, over-business-like, or downright nasty artist. It's not that they're not interested – in general they're pretty well informed. Decisions are carefully weighed, but where the real decisions come from is always left unsaid. They're also the ones who are good at remembering names and events. And they're always friendly and polite to people, not only in the industry, but also to fans. What characterizes them, in fact, is a very high level of involvement with their fans. The guys from the Irish band The Script will nearly always make time for a chat and even Lady Gaga, with her busy schedule, regularly spends hours after her show talking to her fans. Of course, they've got more time for that, because they completely trust the expertise and professionalism of the people around them. You could label the thinker as the ultimate collaborative partner.

4. The shiner
The artist who doesn't want anything to do with anything and just wants to 'shine on the stage'.

There are more of this type than you'd think. Partly because some musicians have no interest in the whole world beyond the stage. I don't mean the orchestral violinist or the drummer who prefers to work in the studio. I mean musicians who've got stage-fever, musicians whose egos need regular stroking. For many of these artists, it's simple: 'I sing and that's what my job is. I don't need to compose. I get a good salary and a nice bit of attention from my fans.' You could call this an easy gig, but you can't actually avoid having to deal with the industry around it. New records need promotion, for example. And although photo sessions might be fun, interview questions can be tricky. Shiners don't really have opinions, they just want to play. And having an opinion can sometimes get in the way of your easy gig. So the shiner is always cheerful and positive, and avoids difficult questions. After all, you can't accidentally admit that old people make you gag. Then you'd lose all your shows in retirement homes.

An added problem for the shiner is their image. It's now accepted that some artists don't write their own songs, but you must have some kind of talent, and I'm not talking about being a good dancer or having a pretty face. Being able to sing well is an absolute requirement, because otherwise before you know it you'll be in the same boat as Milli Vanilli. These two men scored huge worldwide hits. But when the pre-recorded track got stuck during a 'live show', they fell apart and everyone immediately realized that the guys hadn't sung the songs themselves. What followed was public humiliation – besides having to give back all the trophies they had in their cupboards – and it even led to the tragic suicide of one member of the duo. A sad story, and yet you'd be surprised at how many artists there are who still earn their living in exactly the same way. But the artist who just does their thing, a bit of singing and a bit of being cheerful, that's not so very crazy. And these people aren't actually all that bad for the industry. These are the artists who keep managers and record companies nicely busy. After all, the shiner lets the professionals take care of the repertoire and they won't have a stubborn artist contradicting them. In other words, the shiner seems perfect for the industry. And they really are, as long as they have no opinions at all.

Someone once explained to me why the shiner does what he does. To make things easy, let's call the shiner Pete. Pete loves singing and performing and sees these two things as his job. He's not a composer or a multi-instrumentalist, his job is simply singing and performing. And preferably as often as possible. Like going to work.

5. The superstar

The name says it all: the superstar is a perfectly balanced combination of the first four types. And superstars are usually the exception, 'the outside category', as we could call them. They know how everything works and they're nice people, but they don't have to be liked, because they know exactly who they need. These are the people you want to work with, the gamechangers. When these artists want to do something, mountains are moved. There are plenty of examples. Radiohead, who let you decide for yourself what you want to pay for an album. Adele, who releases her record in physical form only and so makes all the streaming platforms wait, for the first few months. Mumford & Sons, who tour with their own festival line-up... All acts that bend the rules of the industry and actually bring about change. Hang on a minute, do they really create major changes? In that case we're forgetting that such changes usually apply only to the superstars, because if you're a new artist and you introduce these kinds of ideas, everyone will have forgotten them by tomorrow. But, fair enough, the superstars do bring about some change!

And if you look at the people round these superstars, you'll see that they're all pretty relaxed. They are well-oiled machines, made up of experienced and professional people. They're people who need no more than a single word to make things happen, and they make things possible instead of frustrating their progress. If at a certain point you reach this level, then you'll get to meet everyone: the security man for One Direction is suddenly also with Adele; you see Bruno Mars' production manager working for BTS; the Arctic Monkeys' manager is also the manager of Royal Blood – that sort of thing. And the artists? Their address books are soon filled with the details of other A-listers. After all, they're all in the same position: influential, hounded by the media, and with plenty of newly acquired wealth. But they're surrounded by people who know what they're talking about, and they're not afraid to learn. The elements they understand (not simply think they understand) are considered seriously and in consultation with others. The rest is filled in by the team, and the artist trusts and relies on them, 100 percent.

As you go along you'll learn how the industry works, little by little, and up to the highest level. With all your accumulated knowledge – which will go much further than reading this book! – you'll have a super-team to work with that can actually set things in motion. I don't think I need to explain that if you want to make it in the music industry you've got to be in the superstar's periphery. But there's still an important lesson for you to learn.

THE ARTIST IS SACRED
(WHILE THEY'RE UNDER CONTRACT)

It feels almost strange to have to explain this, but for the sake of completeness it's perhaps the right thing to do. The artist is sacred, because everything revolves around them. The artist is the person who's got the talent and the image, but if things go wrong, then the artists are the ones who publicly bear the brunt. That seems obvious to me, but it isn't the case that everyone else completely understands this. Commercial entities, for example, still think that if you pay the piper you call the tune. The Rolling Stones were once asked to pretend there was a power cut during a show and then use a fake plug to switch it on again, before launching into 'Start Me Up'. Yes indeed, the sponsor was an energy supplier, and he who pays the piper calls the tune. That seems rather an outdated notion now, but it didn't come from nowhere. When the music industry started, that's precisely how it was. The artist worked for the record company, the producer or the promoter. After all, they were the ones paying the artist's fee or their wages. Yes, that's right: their wages. In the early days, most artists worked for a regular wage. They sang songs and appeared on record sleeves for just a few dollars a month. And if they didn't look good enough, but had a special voice, then someone else would be phoned up for the cover image. Or vice versa.

Promoters took the risks for the show, so they were the employers. The fact that tickets were sold because of the artist didn't come into the equation at all. Promoters weren't only the ones taking the risks, they also made the decisions about the setlist, the length of the show, support acts and so on. So it makes complete sense that these roles have now switched round, almost 100 percent. It makes sense for artists to stand up for themselves. Nevertheless, there are still some genres in which the artist is more a puppet than an authentic creator. In pop music, in particular, artists and groups are still assembled and manufactured, although that seems to be the only genre in which that's publicly accepted. Yet even there you find an urge for authenticity. When those manufactured groups fall apart, several solo careers do remain, although the majority won't be successful. Incidentally, it's often the case that only one member of a group is really successful. But more about that later.

The music industry was once sacred, and now it's the artist. And anyone who denies that isn't telling the truth. And actually that's not so strange at all, as the artist is the one who brings in the money and provides the employment. If the artist doesn't play live, there won't be any ticket revenues. If no music is made, no royalties come in. Put simply: if the artist doesn't play the role of being an artist, then the publishers, promoters, managers, agents, producers, product managers, venues, and all the various support staff will be forced to sit at home, unemployed.

Are artists so sacred that they can do anything then? To a certain extent, yes, but the fact that one person usually represents several artists shows that pressure can be applied. Producers can give their best songs to others, agencies can put you at the bottom of the pile, and record companies can spend their precious time and energy on someone else. But if the artist has a whole series of hits to their name and if the venues keep selling out, then as the music industry you haven't got a leg to stand on. Then you've simply got to bend like a reed in the wind when the artist comes up with yet another silly idea.

IOU

One good turn deserves another. That happens in the music industry too. We call them 'pleasers'.

If you've got a successful artist under contract, you've got power. It's as simple as that. You've got something that others really want: a piece of the pie. And since you've got plenty of choice when it comes to sharing it, you want something valuable in return. First and foremost, you want a good deal. Your job is to get as much as possible out of it for the artist, and the bigger the artist, the easier it is. But something else may also be at play here, something that can cloud the negotiations.

Because things are going so well for you, you get offered other artists. People generally have a tendency to be greedy, and so it won't be long before you're taking care of several artists. Since campaigns don't run all the time, you've often got time in hand, so bearing that in mind you feel you can afford to manage one or more extra artists. Moreover, there's plenty of money coming in, so you can easily employ more staff. And don't forget, you honestly believe that those new acts aren't simply promising, but they're going to be really big stars.

And then something strange happens. You've miraculously forgotten more or less the whole route you first charted out with your successful artist. You still think there's some point in playing the smaller venues (clocking up the miles), but doing promos on regional TV and radio stations is a waste of time and money. You've got a huge network now, you're higher up the ladder, and you can get things done much faster. (You'll discover later that this is also the main reason people want to work with you). And it does seem a lot easier to make things happen. So it's a small step to help your new acquisitions on their way. Your newest talents have really got it made. People take more of what you offer and they're more willing to play the new artist's music. Organizers will be keen to book your acts and most likely put a better deal on the table. Because everything you touch turns to gold!

No, hang on a minute, there's something completely different going on here. Have you ever heard of the IOU principle? This is based on the idea that if you do something for someone, that person owes you something in return. In other words: I'll make sure your act gets a great deal and for that I expect something back. The trick then is to delay the 'paying back' as long as you can. But in fact it's ingrained in people to settle matters as quickly as possible. When the neighbours borrow a cup of sugar from you, you'll see that they'll try to pay you back in the shortest possible time. Either immediately ('I really do want to pay you for this!') or the next day, when you'll get a full packet of sugar in return (with a nice bar of chocolate thrown in).

The IOU principle is used all the time in the music industry. Not surprising, because quite a lot of free stuff is handed out –invites for the show, special album releases, shake & fakes, merchandise, you name it. It's quite easy to keep a record of all that, as it's not all that difficult to keep a list of who you've given what to, and what you got in return. You could even map out the whole pyramid like this, to see where you are in the industry and who still owes you something. But when the dividing line is thinner, and you can't clearly indicate when you're doing someone a favour, it gets a bit more complicated.

To give an example: if an agent books a headliner act for a festival, who is helping whom? The festival is making one of its most desirable slots available, with a fat fee included, so the agent clearly owes the festival something. However, the festival really does want that headliner (because there aren't all that many of them), and although they're paying a lot to get it, the act is well worth it. Besides, the agent could have chosen a different festival. So the festival clearly owes the agent something.

This kind of thinking plays a subconscious role when a festival headliner is being booked and both ways of seeing it contain a grain of truth. So then it comes down to the relationship between the festival and the agent. If the agent has an up-and-coming or struggling artist in their stable, then in many cases they'll try to get them on the festival programme too, using this argument: 'You've got my act as your headliner, and now you owe me a favour in return.' In 95 percent of cases the festival will want to go along with that. But in other cases the festival will try to get another successful artist from the agent's books. They'll use this argument: 'All my budget has gone on the headliner, so I want you to throw in another act as part of the bargain.' If that works, then the game begins again. The agent will say: 'You got a bargain with that act, so I've got another great up-and-coming act you really should book!'

I'll say it again, in practice this is all done without too many words.

Another example: some music is played on certain radio stations for very different reasons than for pure love of the song. Really? Surely the fact that Taylor Swift has promised the station an exclusive interview can't have anything to do with it? Well, perhaps not directly, but if you read between the lines, you'll eventually spot the links.

In the heyday of the music industry, when money was still flooding into the record companies, delegations regularly went on trips abroad. Short trips to Barcelona, London, Norway, or further, all paid for by the company. Jollies, as we called them. The group was usually made up of buyers (from websites or record stores), broadcasting managers, journalists and promoters. It's true that the promoters weren't all that useful in the short-term, but it was always good to demonstrate to an artist that you also took the live element seriously. Payola had been banned for some decades already, so you mustn't think that it was anything like that (i.e. nothing at all like literally paying radio DJs to play a record) but people were certainly pampered.

On a trip to London to see Pixie Lott, who was then a new act, we were travelling with the Free Record Shop's owner and its buyer. This undoubtedly wasn't their first experience of going on a jolly, because during the morning flight to London they very professionally filled themselves up with the best wine on offer. By the time the meet & greet with Pixie Lott was due to happen, they were completely smashed. What followed was the most embarrassing spectacle I've ever seen, certainly one involving an artist and a record retailer. Pixie Lott was so inexperienced and distressed that she had no idea what to do with this very merry record retailer and his accomplice, nor how to handle their crude comments. The photo opportunity just about worked, but you could compare it to seeing a pair of clowns, high on LSD, trying to explain to Queen Elizabeth that they're very popular with the kiddies. And after that we still had to go to the show, where I – completely and utterly sober –

made plans for the artist's future with her agent, while the gentlemen were sleeping off their hangover. And they weren't even all that young anymore. I've never found out how many Pixie Lott albums the Free Record Shop actually bought, but it must have been a lot more than for many other new artists. Unfortunately, Pixie Lott's career never really took off beyond the UK.

But concert organizers can get something out of candy trips too. Journalists are still flown all over the world to write reviews, in the hope that this publicity will sell more tickets for the shows. And radio stations and sponsors send people all over the world to watch sports events. But the question is: how bad is all this? It's an ethical question. In the payola era people were actually paid – privately, in cash or cars – to get something done. I remember having lunch in L.A. with an agent who, after paying the bill, said: 'I've paid your lunch, now get me a show.' Is that blackmail or a rather direct form of IOU?

I'll stick to what's important here, which is keeping your network relevant and up to date, which means that you'll subconsciously take the pros and cons of a collaboration into account. Because in itself, of course, it really isn't bad to do something for someone else every now and then.

What's a bit disappointing, but also puts things into perspective, is that artists who've been helped through the industry as 'pleasers' are often not successful (or not anymore). I believe that success is determined by a number of different factors. One factor is that both parties should get something from it and want something from each other. If an artist really wants to play at a certain festival but the festival doesn't like the look of them, it won't work. If an artist really wants to sign with a particular label, but the label doesn't like the look of them, it won't work. Then you can push your artist onto the festival or the label, as a pleaser, but in practice that won't deliver very good results. The opposite way round doesn't work either. If a festival or label really wants to secure an artist, but the artist doesn't like the look of them, it also won't work. You can swap 'festival' or 'label' with the words 'publisher', 'sponsor', 'promoter', 'booker', 'venue' or any other branch of the music industry, and the results will be the same.

I think this is because of the following: collaboration is the key to success in this industry. Both sides have to do their utmost to reach greater heights. That may sound a little vague, but doing a good job simply isn't good enough. Everything in the music industry connects together through a series of coincidences, so you don't want to deliver half a performance at a crucial moment.

Both sides must have the will to collaborate with each other, even if the partnership is short-lived. Because then they'll go through fire for each other. If a particular label or festival really wants to sign a specific artist, they'll shout out louder about it when they do sign; and the artist will publicly display their strong appreciation for the partnership if they're entirely happy with it. But in the case of 'pleasers' – the acts signed on as a favour – it'll all be shoved under the mat as much as possible, and if anybody says anything about it, it will be implied that the contract was signed under some pressure. The sum is clear: $1 + 1 = 2$, but in the music industry you go for $1 + 1 = 3$. In the case of pleasers, however, you usually end up with $1 + 1 = 0$.

But you mustn't confuse pleasers and support acts (although many people perhaps think they're the same). Support acts are a whole other story and their importance is just as frequently underestimated as overestimated.

SUPPORT ACTS DON'T SELL
(BUT THEY'RE MORE IMPORTANT THAN YOU'D THINK)

The support act has origins of an entirely practical nature, the same as the merchandise deal. The merchandise deal, which means that artists have to give up some of the revenue from selling T-shirts, for example, originates in a practical problem. Because some of the space inside the hall had to be set aside for the sales area, there was less space for the audience. That meant that fewer tickets could be sold and the venue owners wanted compensation. That's why a percentage of the turnover has to be surrendered, till this very day. And nowadays you've got to add something for the sellers, the administration and all the other peripheral matters. But the fact that those sales areas are no longer actually inside the auditorium has been ignored for years.

The support act, in its current form, has come into existence in a similar – yet rather silly – way. The main act didn't usually have enough repertoire for a full set, and the venue owner and the promoter simply wanted to keep the audience inside a little longer. Because the longer an audience is inside the venue, the more they drink and perhaps even have something to eat. And then people take off their coats, make more use of the toilets, and at any rate have more time to spend their money. And if there's more money coming into the venue, the promoter has to pay less for its hire. Of course, saying that the support 'is warming up the audience for the main act' makes a much more interesting story. That sounds a little better when you're asking an artist to be the support. Besides, it's a lot easier to justify the standard 150 euros you'll pay them if you can argue that they're 'going to get the audience geared up for the main act'. That amount is low enough to take on the risks of the venue hire, and not quite so low that it's an insult to the band. For your information: 150 euros will just about cover their van rental.

So why would a band want to be the support act at all? The answer is very simple: reach. You get the chance to play in front of a lot of people. Even if they didn't come there for you, it could well happen that each show will bring you another thirty fans. That doesn't sound a lot perhaps, but if that happens with every show, it might just get the ball rolling in the right direction. Another reason: experience. As a support act you can build up experience in large venues, at a point when you're not yet filling them yourself. The show usually starts with an empty house, but it's nearly always the case that by the end of the support set, the place is pretty full (as long as the ticket sales for the main act have gone well). Let's expand on this a little: as a support act you're probably going to be noticed by people in the music industry. That's a plus point if you're looking for an agent or a record deal, for example. And then there's your biography, that little piece of text that you, your manager or agent will use to try and sell your act. If you've done a series of support acts for famous headliners, that looks good for your story. Of course, it's best if you can be the support for an entire tour, since you'll immediately get international reach, gain more experience, meet many more professionals and get an even better story. You (or the record company or some other investor) just accept that it's going to cost something. But it could be the start of a glittering career!

I could be very cynical about this right now, but instead let me give you some examples of acts that have done support shows. Lady Gaga, for example, was the opener for The Pussycat Dolls. But there are many more examples than this: Prince, Jimi Hendrix, Led Zeppelin, Guns N' Roses, Stevie Wonder, Queen, Rage Against the Machine, Nirvana, Justin Bieber, and Bruno Mars are just a few of the big names who once supported another artist. What would be interesting would be to research these tours in depth to find out if these acts were there as 'pleasers' or simply to increase the artists' reach.

But there has been a development in the history of the opening act. At first the headliners didn't want, or weren't allowed, to interfere with the choice of the warm-up. The venue or promoter chose the support act with the idea that like this they could offer their local artist pals the chance for a great performance. That gets you some credit with them, so that if the act gets a bit bigger, you can ask them again. Luckily, that's still something that sometimes happens. What also sometimes happens is that the tickets for the main act aren't selling well. And if you can't get rid of the tickets, you can always book a local support act with a loyal fanbase. You'll get a full house like that, especially with a generous guestlist too. This strategy must have worked well in the past, which means that now, if a show isn't selling well, every venue and promoter will still get the question: can't you book a support act that sells? I have no idea which acts that may have worked for. I can't name a single one. Yet the idea that this will work seems very deep-seated. When the tickets aren't selling, you still get asked, to this very day: don't you think a local support would sell more tickets?

Well, the only answer is no. Support acts don't sell, it's the main show that sells the tickets. You get the opening act thrown in for free. Compare it to shopping in a supermarket. You do your shopping, go to the till to pay, and then you can choose whether you want stamps or coupons. If you save such things, you can take advantage, but you don't have to. It's a nice bonus if it's a good special offer, but it's no problem at all if it's not included in the total package. And that's because no one really knows who these support acts are. Yes, if we'd known back then that Nirvana was going to be really big, of course, more tickets would have sold when they were the support act. But if we'd known that, we wouldn't have needed the headliner either.

That's something I always find funny about festivals that claim they booked an artist in the early stages, before the artist became internationally known and got a much bigger audience. 'You-know-who performed here a few years back, so we're a really cool festival.' Yeah. All very nice, but that was when you-know-who was a complete unknown, and no one knew yet that we'd all think they're really great. And now you just can't book them anymore, so every year we watch unknown acts that might break through. But maybe they won't, so what's the point? We want to see really cool acts at your festival that have just made a breakthrough. But that seems to be difficult, because no one knows exactly when an act breaks through.

So, those agents and managers who still think you can sell a few more tickets with a support act are hopelessly out of date. Actually, they still believe in fairy tales. I can honestly say that in almost twenty-five years in the live industry I've never yet booked a support act that suddenly made the ticket sales go through the roof. But what needs to be added is that if you're going to book a support act for the sake of ticket sales, that usually only happens when the ticket sales have already started. It is, of course, impossible to calculate the difference that supports acts would make to sales if you announced them right away.

I'll say a little more about the development and history of supports, because there has certainly been an evolution in recent years. It's changed from not wanting or being allowed to know anything about supports, to: 'We're the artists and we've got some pals who'd like to tour with us.' And that's what happened: there's been an explosion in the number of support acts brought along by the artists themselves. At first that started as a favour among friends, but of course there was always some failed manager or business partner who thought they could cash in on this. And that was the point at which paying to be the support act was introduced. That meant that the headliner was paid to take a support on tour, and the production costs that the support tour created were usually added. Travel and accommodation costs, the costs for lighting and sound, such as having their own mixing desks, catering. That soon mounts up, but it can be well worth the investment. Not only does the support get a very large reach, but you can promote them at the same time, and that will save a few extra flights and hotels.

Yet this pay-to-play model turned out to be a bridge too far and it's gone very quiet in that area in recent years. What seems to be the trend at the moment is that the headliner wants to make it a great evening with a support that gives credibility and positivity to the main act. 'Hey! See what cool acts we can take on tour with us!' So, fortunately, the new generation of artists seems to be going for a total package, a great night out with great music. And I know what you must be thinking – yes, those support acts do indeed get much more than 150 euros.

YOU'VE GOT TO BLAME SOMEONE

Imagine: you're a music artist. Or perhaps you really are an artist, and you don't have to imagine it. That's fine too.

You've got a glittering career, not a cloud in the sky. Your songs are all near the top of the streaming charts. You're even managing to sell CDs, cassette tapes and LPs. The live recording breaks all the records and even the DVD stays in the hit charts. In short: everything's going smoothly, but you're also working really hard for that. No indulging in excesses, no one knows that you've got a covert boyfriend or girlfriend. And that secret relationship with your childhood friend is something that even your manager doesn't know about, so your image can't be damaged. The money's flooding in and plenty of good deals have been made. Your manager knew you from back in the day and will never sell you short, in brief: everything is going perfectly and everyone is happy. You're at the top of the peak, and no one can push you off.

It's time for a new record, and you've invested a lot of energy into finding a producer and a co-writer. You've put the perfect team together, with new musicians for the recording studio and the tour (slightly more expensive than the previous team, but they're much better too), and you get down to work. In fact, once the songs are there, you've got so many that there's more than enough for the record. So you'll be spoilt for choice. As there's a large budget, it all fits nicely into the picture. The recordings are brilliant and you're as happy as a kid in a candy store. It's time for the first bump in the road: what will the manager think? Actually, he can't wait to start selling it. He's totally convinced of its quality and so he starts the new round of negotiations with the record company, full of fire. And the record company also realizes that the record is much better than they expected. An even better deal! And what's more, the set of songs they're interested in perfectly matches what you think. So you were right! The agent is very soon instructed to book larger venues and to ask for higher fees, and that's easily done, given the past ticket sales and the high expectations.

When the first single is released everyone's on the same page and far more has been invested in it than was initially intended. But hey, it's not easy to get your hands on gold in this industry! And this one really isn't a risk. This is the definite breakthrough and you – the artist – are sure of that too, because even your lawyer and your accountant think it's great, and they never take risks!

The success of the first single is so huge that it's even a hit in other countries. What no one expected to happen is actually happening, and not on a small scale either. It was already going well, it could certainly go better, but now it's going through the roof. You fly all over the world to chat to the local media about the single and how well it's doing. And there's still the album to come! And the publisher is watching the money come in by the bucketful!

Every radio station is playing the record and advertising agencies are fighting for the right to use the song in their ads. The agent has to think hard now, because the deals were good and the venues were large, but with this success they'll probably be too small. The festivals that were booked have got the act too cheaply. Shouldn't the fees be raised? And the fans will surely understand if some local festivals are switched for a few international ones.

And then comes the date of the release of the second single, and the fabulous next album. Although the date has been changed once already because 'the first single is still doing so well.' Anyway you can't bring out a second single when the first is still at the top of the charts. After much deliberation, the album and the second single are released three weeks later than planned. All the interviews have been published and your release party was a huge celebration. The reviews of the album are fairly positive, but the new single doesn't get much of a chance on the radio. After all, they're still playing the first one every day. The reactions from your fans to the album are admittedly a little grumpy, but there's nothing for you to worry about as yet. You do hear some muttering about you 'getting too big now', 'going for the big money', 'suddenly playing the big venues instead of intimate shows', but those sorts of comments are probably exceptions.

And then the festival season comes along, combined with the release of your third single. You're playing on the big stages now, not in those cosy tents where you can still see the audience up close. No more than a few yards between the stage and the audience. You do still recognize some fans from the previous tour in the distance, but actually most faces in the audience are new. And it's a different kind of audience too, suddenly a lot more mothers, housewives and computer nerds. Very different from the cool kids you're used to. But hey, fans are fans! It's just a bit strange that everyone runs off to other stages right in the middle of the set, after you've played the hit. Fortunately, a handful of diehard fans are still there to support you, although not more than 30 percent of what was first there. The diehards are still swaying along with your latest single, but it won't ever be a real hit. Because fewer people at your show means less attention, and so fewer sales. You comfort yourself with the thought that no one ever buys a record in the summer anyway.

Once you're back from festival life, it's time to get ready for the tour. The festival shows should have given an extra boost to the ticket sales, but unfortunately that didn't work out. Perhaps it wasn't such a good idea to book the tour so soon after the festival. It's not possible to cancel it, because the investments have already been made and the tour sponsor will ask for their money back. The money isn't there anymore and – more importantly – cancelling a tour will create quite some loss of face. And if people get to hear that the tour isn't going ahead because of poor ticket sales, you'll get a lower fee next time. You don't want to end up in a downward spiral. So the tour carries on. The promoters are losing a lot of money from the shows and are doing all they can to get the venues full. And to the paying fans' dismay, it even seems they're throwing free tickets around. An additional problem is that the atmosphere during the shows isn't great. This makes for lukewarm reactions and poor merchandise sales. The people from the record company don't even dare to shake hands in the dressing room, because they're scared of being confronted by a frustrated act. And to cap it all, tensions are running high among the crew members, because the budget has almost gone. In fact, in hindsight it's obvious that this tour didn't bring a great result either.

Then it's time for a fresh start and a new album. But the record company doesn't have a workable budget available anymore. It isn't possible to generate income with a new tour, because you were at all those festivals last year without much success. The venues can't see the point of a new show either, because there's no new material. In other words: your career is melting away, like snow in the sun.

Who's to blame?

The manager
The manager is the project leader and the person in control. He should have intervened much earlier when things started going wrong and put his foot down. But he was too busy working for that other artist, so too little energy was invested in this project. In the end it boils down to this: the process wasn't properly managed. Yes, it's the manager's fault.

The producer
The producer may have sensed exactly what was on trend, but they didn't show enough grit with the second and third single. You can't come up with the same sound twice. Everyone knows that! That's something the fans will never accept and the radio stations certainly won't. The producer should have come up with more creative input, so it's their fault that the artist's career is over.

The publisher
The publisher should never have teamed up with all those commercial parties. All those movies, games and ads made the first single so huge that everyone got sick of the song and the artist. The publisher would have been better off holding back, doing something with arthouse films instead of blockbusters, and they should never have provided the music for that violent game. That doesn't suit the artist's image at all, the publisher should have realized that. The publisher is clearly to blame.

The record company
The biggest culprit. They kept the second single back, which meant that the timing was wrong for radio stations and it didn't get any airplay. And they didn't do enough promo at the festivals and shouldn't have released a full album, but should have tested the water with two EPs. Anyway, it's completely ridiculous that they don't want a new contract with the artist, because they made plenty of dough from the first single. It actually looks like they want to wash their hands of the artist because they've

signed a new act that's seven years younger and who'll do everything the record boss tells them. Even if they weren't bringing a Gold Record, the company's local offices could have dropped in on the shows. Oh yes, if anyone has killed this career, it's the record company.

The agent
The wrong bookings, for the wrong festivals – and if the festival was good, it was the wrong time or the wrong stage. And that tour started way too soon after the festivals. And the venues were too big. Doesn't everyone know that fans don't have any money after the summer? And it was a waste of money playing criss-cross all over Europe and the money for that well-paid gig in Dubai hasn't come in yet. And touring smaller venues as was suggested, may have been a good idea, but taking the whole crew wouldn't have been financially viable, and it really won't work with fewer people. Now the venues don't want the show anymore as consumer confidence has vanished, simply because a few tickets were given away. No live career means no career at all: the agent is the one who did it!

The accountant and the lawyer
They completely misjudged it. They should never have agreed to all that expense. How can you agree to everything the tour manager demands? Okay, the tour manager may say that this is what the artist wants, but who's supposed to keep an eye on things? Five star hotels! Couldn't they have been one or two stars less? And why did we pay for all that booze for all those pals? Didn't they have any money of their own? And why did the publisher, the agent and the record company get such high percentages? Couldn't they have made a better deal? The career's gone down the drain and the money's finished. Oh yes, the accountant and the lawyer are to blame.

The artist
No, it isn't the artist's fault. You can't blame them for anything. Because: the artist is sacred. You knew that, didn't you?

A GIRL IN EVERY PORT

It's addictive, that urge for contact with artists. But why is there such a strong desire to meet them? You even have a business model that plays on that, in the form of meet & greets. I think it's to do with the idea that if you share something of yourself with the artist, you'll get something from the artist in return.

But what happens after a first meeting? Then you want to see the artist again and most of all you want the artist to recognize you. You want to leave as much of an impression on them as they've made on you.

Perhaps you know the saying: 'A girl in every port.' Let's dip into this a bit. The Musician does an extensive first tour and has an affair in every town they play. A kind of holiday boyfriend or girlfriend, and that's easy enough, because the act isn't very famous yet and they're managing the tour themself. But it all becomes a little more complicated with the next tour, because the shows are somewhat bigger and it's more difficult for the fans to get in. And anyway, there are always a few fans you'd really like to see, but also quite a few that you wouldn't. There are some fans who actually want to travel along with you for a while, but that's a bit complex in terms of planning. So you try to pass that on to your new tour manager, but he's not totally crazy so he just leaves you floundering for a bit. All the same, things are still going pretty well, just two or three awkward scenes and a handful of 'we forgot to put you on the guestlist' excuses. In this way you can still get away with it. But then comes the third tour: the big venues. Your own manager, a production manager, tour manager and security. Oh, and yes, a partner... The location of the hotel is jealously guarded, even by you, but the paparazzi keep following you everywhere, so it's hard to be discreet. The result: farewell to 'a girl (or boy) in every port', farewell to that endless list of fun on every tour.

This may all sound a bit dramatic and it's certainly a somewhat dated way of talking about the joys of a tour. Anyway, when it comes to secret relationships nowadays, they won't go down well on social media, so it seems that the whole concept of 'a girl in every port' has been squashed even before you've got those first kilometres under your belt. Though I'm sure there are creative ways to get round it. You've got plenty of single record company employees, for example, who treat the term 'business relationship' very freely, and whole books could be written about this by the assistants of (novice) agents. But to get to the heart of the matter, I actually mean something completely different by the term 'a girl in every port'. I'm not a neurologist and I certainly don't have any understanding of the brain, but I'd say that it's something to do with memory trace cells. I mean the cells involved in neural firing patterns, which play an important part in memory retrieval.

In short, and very roughly, it comes down to the fact that the mind stores memories in small fragments, such as the location where something happened, for example. When you're at that location again, your brain cells are apparently triggered into specific firing patterns, which are similar to previous moments in that place. But what's the point of all this amateur science to you? Well, it could explain why if you usually work in a fixed place (such as a specific city or country) you will be recognized by the artist if you're there, whereas if you're in some random other place, they won't recognize you. That's not so strange. As an artist you have to deal with – roughly speaking – one manager, one A&R manager, one product manager, one agent, and one lawyer. These are the people that take care of your affairs for the whole world. Let's say you have twenty focus countries in Europe. If you're doing a promotion in each of those countries, then that's twenty local product managers just in Europe, and if you add in all their promotion managers, you've got to remember forty people. These people all work really hard for you, so you do at least want to know them by name. Fortunately, you also get to tour those countries after all that promotion. Then you'll get another twenty promoters, probably all with their own assistants and marketeers. On average, forty more people who are working their guts out for you. Then the publishers, who are also doing their very best for you in each country, just like the journalists and media people who helped you so much or reviewed you so well when you started. So that's another eighty people or so. Then add the girl, or boy, in every port from your first tour and all the friends you made early on, in bars and other venues. Your sum total in Europe is at least a hundred and fifty people, all of whose names you're supposed to remember.

And that's just in Western Europe, because you've got to cope with an endless number of states in the US and all those difficult names in the Eastern world. Now add alcohol and drug use and you'll understand that it's not so surprising that artists have some difficulty remembering faces and names. So don't be astonished if there are artists or managers who greet you as a best friend in your own territory, but not outside it. Or at least that they need a little help with a brief reminder of who you are. So when you're on unknown ground, i.e. somewhere you haven't ever been before, it's really not such a bad idea to approach an artist you know with the words: 'Hey! It's me, from Holland!', or from wherever you happen to be. Then they can always reply: 'Yeah, I know. Great to see you!' Then everyone's happy.

IT'S ALL GOT TO CHANGE

In films and in television series butlers are always the ones who turn out to be the murderer, or else the most trusty and loyal servants. The butler is the main character's righthand man, standing in his shadow and making sure that everything is perfectly arranged, exactly as desired. One of the most loyal butlers on record is Alfred, Batman's faithful servant, who has been at his side since he was a little bat-child. It's no coincidence that Alfred's official surname is Beagle – yes, that breed known to be the most loyal dog in the world.

It's just to be expected that if you work in the music industry you'll sometimes feel like a butler. But it will seem impossible to you that your loyalty won't be returned. Because if you're looking after a successful artist and giving them all you've got – time, soul and ultimate salvation – then of course you'll get something in return. Financial compensation is, hopefully, not usually the problem – you will of course have agreed on a percentage, or you're working for a salary. No, where the tension lies is in the field of influence and trust. If you've been working with an artist for a long time, then a bond develops between you that starts looking like a form of equality. That's a really good sign, in theory, as long as everyone bears in mind that all the parties involved are good at one specific thing. And that people should only focus on their own expertise. And that's tricky, because you also want to develop, to learn more, and become better in other fields that don't necessarily fit your talents. And besides you're there already, next to all the action, so if you've got to learn something somewhere, you may just as well do that in the lion's den.

Careers inevitably have high and low points, and if you go through all those stages with the artist, you can't help but move towards friendship instead of just a business relationship. You trust each other with the biggest secrets, you even visit people's homes and build bonds with members of their family. All really intense and crazy, but when the flag is not flying so cheerily anymore, then in the music industry you're suddenly on your own again. A time will come when the idea crops up: we've got to do everything differently, and in particular without you. As we saw earlier, that won't change much, or anything at all, but still the idea is that things will turn around or success will be more likely with another team. Maybe you didn't realize this would happen and you were relying far too much on that comfy bed of yours. Perhaps you should have been a touch more proactive or have come up with more innovative ideas. But it's almost inevitable that at some point there'll be a break-up. Whatever the reason may be, when a business decision suddenly becomes very personal it hits you hard.

For example, right from the start of his career, I was the promoter in the Netherlands for the Belgian singer-songwriter Admiral Freebee – from rising talent to established name and welcome guest in the music world. Over the years I got him into the whole Dutch live circuit – the biggest festivals and the smallest clubs, from just a few people in the house to sold-out tours. In those thirteen years I saw at least four managers come and go, and at least three record labels released the new music, but as far as shows in the Netherlands were concerned there was always one steady element: and that was me, the promoter. My children were given bathrobes, embroidered with their names, and they wore their Admiral Freebee T-shirts with pride. But after fourteen years I heard by chance that from that time on all the bookings would go through my colleague. Yes, you've understood correctly: I didn't hear from that colleague that I'd been axed, nor from the manager or the artist. I was told by the local promoter of a particular venue that the act was now with a different manager and a new promoter.

To this very day I've heard nothing more from the artist, although the new manager once promised me that I'd be phoned at some point. What was the reason? We'd played several times at every festival in the Netherlands, and had seen every venue. Had the enthusiasm vanished or had I been too negative? Was it perhaps a breath of fresh air they wanted? Was it me or was it them? I have no idea. They've never explained it to me. And it really doesn't matter, because there isn't a good reason anyway. It's just that the trust has gone and in the music industry that means: 'Make way for someone else, because it's all got to change.'

NEVER WORK WITH YOUR IDOLS

Some people are simply better than others. You'll hear plenty of clichés about our basic sameness, because 'You know, those stars have to use the toilet every day just like us'; or 'Hey, we're all actually equal', but in my opinion these are utter nonsense. If I compare myself to Katy Perry, she really can sing better than me. Bruno Mars is without a shadow of doubt the better entertainer, and I'm convinced that Dave Grohl can play the guitar much better than I can. I'm absolutely sure that the world sees it like this too, and that's why all three of them have done so well. What's more, they've acquired their (intellectual) wealth both through their hard work and their innate qualities. That's why, when we look at the pyramid, artists have a much, much higher position than mere mortals or fans. Of course, you can compare artists with each other, and then you'll see that one artist can do this better and the other is better at that, but you won't have to look far to find plenty of differences between the top and bottom of the pyramid. There is just a small number of people with more talent and capacity than the ordinary citizen and they've traded a normal, decent life for a job in the public eye. That means that everyone has an opinion about them.

There's a price to be paid for showing off your talents. See it as selling your soul to the devil. In exchange for attention, power and money you have to be the best all the time and always perform at your peak, while ordinary folk think everything just comes naturally to you. Great job, superstar! So many people would just love to stand in your shoes.

Which brings us to the fact that many people in the music industry would also like to be a bit of a star. Eccentric behaviour is nothing unusual in this profession and the urge to hang around where the stars are is strong. And don't on any account stop yourself from doing that. But only if you really do have star qualities yourself. Nothing is more embarrassing than someone from the industry who's always wanting to get photographed with artists of all kinds.

There was a little game we played once that got a bit out of hand: 'Let's see who can get the most meetings with Liam Gallagher'. It was probably pretty childish, and when Gallagher realized that we didn't actually play in a band, it stopped being fun for him. And perhaps the comment 'You're the best Beatle I've ever met' also had something to do with it.

Sometimes it's painfully obvious how sick the music industry can be. There was a show in Norway that was delayed by an hour at the last minute because some 'important guests' hadn't yet started their dessert. The house was packed with four hundred fans who'd been waiting for the artist for hours. Well, next time you'll know what the real reason could be when they tell you there's a so-called 'technical problem'.

It really can be difficult not to act like a complete show-off when you're around the stars. But my own attitude is usually a little more restrained. I think it's better to behave a bit more modestly and let my actions do the work for me. That's how to get the respect from the stars that everyone seems to want.

So you're not one of those show-offs and you're not hoping to make friends with the stars? Maybe you're just impressed by a couple of acts? Perhaps you're even a fan? Well, try to avoid them as much as possible and whatever you do, don't make business agreements with them. There's a chance that in real life they'll be a huge disappointment and that will ruin your appreciation for them and their music. Moreover, you'll make the worst deals with artists you're a fan of. You'll overestimate the ticket or record sales, you'll predict too much airplay and buy in too much merchandise. It will all be much too optimistic. Try explaining this calmly to your favourite artist when the venue is less than a quarter full. Try telling them, dry-eyed, that there's a huge financial loss, but you still firmly believe in the artist's career. That belief is worthless if it hasn't been correctly translated into realistic decision-making.

Music is a personal experience, which can evoke emotions and inexplicable feelings at the strangest of moments. That's hard to combine with the toughness and professionalism expected of you in the music industry in this day and age. Be careful not to let the vagaries of the industry ruin your enjoyment of music. Believe utterly in your heroes and help them out as much as you can. But if you want to keep enjoying their music, it's better to worship your idols than to work with them.

PART 3

THE ACT

The act is an element of a role that is being played. This role is performed according to a predetermined pattern.

How do the systems of the music industry work?
What are its unwritten rules for creating added value?

IT'S NOT ABOUT THE MONEY,
IT'S ALL ABOUT THE MONEY

Music and money don't make a good match. That's how the outside world sees it and the fans as well. Although actors and actresses, sportsmen and sportswomen can get away with displaying their expensive tastes, musicians have to show that they're at one with their audience. 'He's still so completely normal'. That sort of thing. There are, of course, exceptions to this – you're not supposed to be broke if you're in hip-hop, for example.

Musicians are renowned for spending everything they have on drink, drugs and extravagant parties and, therefore, for never actually having much money. And in the early days it really was like that – when the managers and record companies were still in charge and pocketed most of the earnings. To take an example from the live music scene, there's a well-known story about the Godfather of Soul that makes my point. James Brown had been booked by a promoter for a venue that could seat 400 people.

The deal was made: 250 dollars for a ninety-minute show. The artist confirmed and when the tickets went on sale, they sold like hot cakes. As a good businessman, and seeing that James Brown's popularity was clearly growing, the promoter thought it best to switch the show to a nearby venue that could take 2,500 people. In no time at all, the extra tickets also sold out. This was a success story in advance, and when James started performing nothing could go wrong. 2,500 frenzied fans and a fantastic show, that's what happened.

But when James Brown's manager went to get the payment, he looked a little less happy. The promoter's contract clearly stated that the performer would get 250 dollars. There was nothing in it about what would happen if more tickets were sold. The promoter stuck strictly to the contract and, after a euphoric show and a sold-out evening, James Brown went home with just 250 dollars. Yes, that's right, and he had to pay his band and crew from that too.

They say that this was the turning point in the live music industry, that this is when managers and performers slowly started swapping their roles. After all, the artist is and has the product, so they're the ones generating the most revenue. But it's not at all strange that performers at the start of their careers are more relaxed about this. Everyone's working their way up and as things are nowadays you can think yourself lucky if there's a recording contract on the table at all. So then it makes sense to agree to a somewhat worse deal.

But when the going gets better and all kinds of people are clustered around an artist, needing to live off their earnings, then the vested interests start getting bigger. And when those interests get bigger, you notice how there are suddenly even more people involved with the performer's career. But mainly you notice that these people take a harder line, in financial terms too.

That's not really surprising: you see the same sort of thing happening with new companies. When you begin, it's still all fun and games, but when the real money starts rolling in, then investors queue up to give you a helping hand. The deals are stronger, the contracts are more comprehensive, and the language is firmer. And it's not so different in the music industry.

But as far as the outside world is concerned not much changes, if things are going well. The performer still looks the same – because that's really what they're like – and they behave exactly as they always did. That's because performers are not meant to be seen as greedy, money-grubbing creatures. If you're the fan of someone who's built a top company from scratch, it's to do with the respect you have for them and their actions. But if you're a musician's fan, then you're a fan of the whole person and their music. You're not their fan because they strike good business deals. I could, of course, mention some exceptions: artists with their own brand of shoes, like Katy Perry, or with their own vodka brands, like Sean Combs and Ludacris. And what about Fenty Beauty, Rihanna's cosmetics collection, or Lady Gaga's make-up, produced by the Haus of Gaga? But it's really not at all surprising that the traditional music industry is suspicious about this development. To what extent does an established artist still need the music industry, if they can get their revenue from completely different sources?

IT'S A BAD DEAL?
(IT'S MUCH WORSE FOR YOUR COMPETITORS)

Once we start talking about deals and agreements, it's time to switch off the canned laughter, because we're now talking about serious matters. So brace yourself, although we'll start light-heartedly.

A good deal is a deal that enables both parties to come out with benefits. See it as being like two sumo wrestlers who can only win the competition when they're both perfectly placed in the middle of the ring. If one of them falls outside the ring, then effectively both have lost. One heavy guy shoves at the other, but isn't allowed to push too hard. The other wrestler shoves back, and ideally doesn't push too hard either. After some pushing back and forth, they both end up in the centre of the ring, where they haggle a little about the details, and then you've got the perfect deal. Both parties have won. Simple, but negotiating is basically nothing more than that. You can make it more complicated by having multiple parties at the table, by squeezing a mediator in between them, or by digging in your heels. Fine. But the basic principle stays the same: two (or more) parties have to meet each other in the middle.

It's important to know why you want to make a deal, and in the music industry the reason is relatively simple: you want a piece of the pie. As already explained in the chapter about the pyramid: the artist is at the top, he, she or they (singular or plural) are 'the hen that lays the golden eggs', and everyone wants a share of that gold. And in exchange the artist will get something back that he, she, or they can't sort out or solve by themselves. But: the manager wants the biggest possible percentage of the biggest income possible. The record label wants to hand over the smallest possible percentage to the artist. The agent wants to earn as much as possible from the live revenues the artist generates, and so on and so forth.

Now you've got this information and the playing field is already clearer. Things will now slowly become more fun. Because the bigger the artist, the higher the revenues. But the pieces of pie do get smaller.

Are you actually aware of your own negotiating position? That makes quite a bit of difference when you're making a deal. A brief example: an act with no songs, no live reputation, no network, record deal or agent hasn't got much to negotiate with, from a business point of view. So what will this artist give to take part in the big game played by successful musicians, to get the chance of achieving megastar status and all the wealth that accompanies that? It doesn't need any complicated sums to realize that such an artist will agree more quickly to giving away a large piece of their pie.

Artists who have independently released one or more successful songs, and have therefore gained a lot of followers, are already in a much better negotiating position. Record companies or promoters are no longer the autocrats they once were. After all, they've got plenty of competitors in the search for successful, rising talent with a growing fanbase (i.e. there's plenty of competition when it comes to acquiring financially interesting investments). In cases like this, negotiations are approached very differently. So, when negotiating, you've definitely got to be aware of your own position.

We've already discussed another important commandment of the music industry: sharing the profits never made anyone poorer. You also need to keep this in mind when you're negotiating. If there's money to be made, naturally you can keep it all for yourself, but you can also share out the profits. Once you start thinking about the amount of work you do, or the risks you're taking, and balance that against the sharing, then your negotiations may suddenly take a very different turn.

A hypothetical example: an artist has recorded and paid for their own record. A record company executive is interested in it and signs a contract with the artist giving both parties 50 percent of the revenue. The agreement is that the record company will just do the promotional work. That's handy for the artist, because then they don't have to do anything else. Handy for the record company, because they already do that sort of thing as part of their daily business. However, in return for half of the record label's revenue, the record company executive finds someone who'll do all the work externally. This party has to take the risk that there may possibly be no revenue at all. A strange scenario? Not in the music industry. Because without having to make much of an effort, the record company will get a nice 25 percent. All that the company executive has to do is make the deal and occasionally tell the artist that the posters really will be all over town tomorrow!

Back to the piece of pie and an important starting point: assume that if someone wants to work with you, you've got something the other person doesn't have, but would like to have. And if they've already got it, then you're better at it, or have got a better version. Without any idea of what you can actually do – or with the idea that you can't do it anyway – it's hard to talk to people. You have to be convinced that your 'goods' or expertise are of sufficient interest and it's a good idea to give that impression when you start selling them. That demands a degree of arrogance, but on the other hand, as the saying goes: who dares wins.

So, we've established that you've got something to offer and that the other party needs what you've got. This is when the tug-of-war can start and, as long as neither party puts their foot in it, you'll most likely end up 'in the middle'. And in the music industry that's called the 'rock 'n' roll deal'. Does the artist want a much higher fee than you're prepared to offer? Is the exploitation period of a record longer than you want to give away? Is the royalty percentage disproportionate? Then it's a question of 'Let's settle in the middle.' Then the deal is made exactly between one side's offer and the other's. And no more complaining after that: if this form of consensus has worked – what we Dutch call the polder model – it means the deal's done and both parties are happy. It's the quickest way to get on with the job at hand without any conflicts.

This all sounds easy, but unfortunately quite a few golf course deals are no longer made the rock 'n' roll way. That's because more people in the music industry are getting better informed about the various sources of income, and so deals are often made at daggers drawn.

I'll clarify this with an example. Let's imagine that there's a manager of a major act and that they're also the promoter in their own country. In their role as manager they make deals with the record companies and when the agent comes along with a budget, they're acting more like a promoter. If this is the way you've been working for a while, you'll have seen every side of the music industry before you start making choices.

That leads to the second, and perhaps most important point: the lack of trust inside the music industry. People have the constant feeling that they're being 'screwed'. And seeing that no one wants to go down in history as a terrible dealmaker, everyone reads up on the different types of 'screwing'. Everyone knows about the record companies that still include packaging costs (for example, printing costs for the cover) in digital downloads. Every manager knows that at concerts they've got to pay more for... – well, whatever – than they should, and every agent knows that the touring company is sneakily earning a bit on the side via the mileage allowance. Still, all these inventive sources of income only evolved because no one trusted anyone else. The percentage of the profits only goes up (or down) because everyone's convinced that the other party is wrongfully generating so much income at the artist's, agent's, record company's or promoter's expense that someone's bound to be the victim. And that's something that no one will ever let happen. However, the lower your place in the pyramid, the less chance you have for a bit of flexibility in your negotiations. Or, simpler still: the less you have to offer – for example because there's a lot of competition in your area – the more difficult it will be to settle on a somewhat reasonable deal.

And now we've reached the nub of this chapter: no deal means no income. Even a bad deal is better for your enterprise than no deal at all. That's why a bad deal's much worse for your competitor. If *you* have the deal, they've got no deal at all. Nevertheless, for one of the two parties the margins are steadily decreasing. And that's the way it goes, again and again.

Technically speaking, I could present this as a diagram, but I think I can just as easily sketch it out in words. It takes the form of a downward spiral. If people keep doing more work for less money, or for lower percentages, you'll end up with only the big, listed companies who just want to keep the train running. Because in the long run it doesn't matter if you lose money on a single show or record, as long as you get enough compensation at the end of the day to balance the books.

And now we're getting to the final destination, the place where people earn their income, with every good intention. How low can you actually drop your margins? Now is the ideal moment to take a reality check, whether consciously or not. If you've made too many bad deals along the way, it's easy to be lured into lying or cheating. And yet, honesty really can be the best policy.

HONESTY IS THE BEST POLICY

The most obvious principle is apparently the hardest to put into practice. There's just one thing that artists want and that's honesty. And, if possible, based on a wealth of experience. Because although every artist wants to be surrounded only by yes-men, at whatever cost, in the end that starts being boring and doesn't lead to any objective decisions – and those are sometimes very necessary.

But it's problematic, the rest of the pyramid has to earn a living from what the artist earns, so why go out of your way to contradict him or her? Why tell the truth, or better still, why tell the whole truth? And there's the rub. There are some things an artist doesn't need to know, just as a manager, record label or agent doesn't need to know everything either. What's the good of the record company knowing that the artist is secretly attracted to people of their own sex, for example? Why tell the agent that the artist stuffs kilos of cocaine up their nose (at their own expense)? And why does the artist have to know that there's a terrible photo that's not going to be used anyway, because then there'd be a years-long ban on interviewing the artist? Okay, technically speaking the sexual orientation is going to reveal itself anyway, the agent has long known that there's a drug problem (and probably joins in the same game too) and those photos will also mysteriously come to light. The problem is that no one in the industry knows when the sludge will be dredged up, so you'd better hope it won't be on your watch and that you won't be held responsible.

In the music industry you're valued for your degree of honesty. And that you sometimes say something you shouldn't have said is just part of the deal. The most important lesson to remember is to do with your timing: never be honest before a show or a recording begins. If you are, then a bad show or record inevitably follows. Without exception. Because being honest actually means holding a mirror up to someone. Of course, you may think everything's fantastic and very honestly go around telling everyone that too, but being honest is actually to do with your critical view of things, and artists definitely need that. They'll get plenty of compliments from their yes-men. It's to do with the hard truth, the dots on the i's that make all the difference. The design of a tour, or the credibility of the songs, that's where you can still have a good effect.

Adele, for example, threw the first version of her third album in the waste bin because two people in her team were honest with her. The songs didn't come from her heart, they came across as being much too manufactured. What you need to know is that Adele isn't someone who finishes a new album quickly. But when there's one in the offing, everyone's eager to release it, because then the money machines will print at full speed again. So you've got to be pretty smart to tell Adele: 'Sorry, your album isn't good enough. Start again.' Because that slows down the whole machinery by at least a year, just when you were hoping to buy a new boat. Unfortunately, we'll never know if this really happened – after all, when an album's released a good story is worth its weight in gold – but if it's true, it supports the old adage: honesty is the best policy. Because that third album was praised to high heaven and turned out to be a huge success.

So is it really so difficult to be honest? And how bad is the music industry in that respect?

I've already talked about how the mistrust between various parties can run pretty high. But contracts were invented to make things a little easier. Though, of course, contracts aren't for signing.

CONTRACTS AREN'T FOR SIGNING

Contracts are the most boring element of the whole industry and I would advise everyone to spend as little time on them as possible. Of course, it is useful to set a few things on paper – that is called a deal memo, as a rule – or, even better, write an email with some details of the agreement. Contracts take all the fun out of the work and they waste loads of time and money because, naturally, you have to hire legal experts to chew over all that dry-as-dust stuff and then spit it out again. By the way, this isn't a sneer about the work of lawyers and legal experts. They're very necessary people. But the legal element doesn't make things any more enjoyable.

Contracts are there to be ignored; you really mustn't sign them. If someone sends you a contract, you can answer as follows: 'Many thanks for the contract. We'll take a look at it and will get back to you asap.' In that way you can put off signing it for a while. And if the other side really starts badgering you about it, you can always add and cross out so many things that they'll be busy checking it for weeks. Nevertheless, there are a few basic principles.

Who
Who does this contract involve?

The date
It's important to have the date of the performance in writing, especially if you're booking shows or a tour. If a single date in a tour is incorrect, all the planning will fall to pieces. With album releases, it's also always best to agree on the release date.

The location or the area
That's something clearly relevant for touring, i.e. knowing where you'll be playing. But it's also useful to be clear about this in the record industry, or with publishers or sponsors, so you know precisely in which territory you're allowed to sell the music.

The financial deal
Perhaps the most important point to have in writing. What will be the financial compensation for the service provided?

The length of the agreement
Or what is the duration of the deal? With shows, that's usually after the last song finishes. With recordings, rights or merchandise it's handy to agree on the end date.

These are the most important elements. Of course, all the rest could be relevant too, but if you trust each other a little, then you won't need any of it. Entire pages are filled with things like 'Make sure that the stage doesn't collapse', or 'You are not allowed to destroy the albums without the artist's permission.' These are all things that in any case will cause a lot of trouble when things go off the rails. Because that's what contracts are made for: to make sure your stuff is as much in order as possible if everything goes to pieces. But if it does go to pieces, both sides immediately lose. Because if you have to pull a contract out of the filing cabinet, then the relationship is already ruined. The moment you can't come to an immediate, workable solution and you have to refer to each line and letter of the agreement, then all confidence in a good outcome has vanished.

The following incident shows that this isn't necessary. I was still part-owner of a record label called Alien Do God. We'd struck a deal with the Swedish indie rock band Caesars Palace. They weren't a minor band when the record was released and already had a number of potential hits. Sales were going well, the shows were great and their career was on the way up. With the third album, which I think followed the first and second albums within a year, it looked as if there was a breakthrough. The single got good exposure on the radio and the band was beginning to be noticed by international record labels. It didn't take long till the major international company EMI knocked at our door to buy back the rights. Of course, we thought that was a shame for us, but it was much better for the band. A worldwide deal could mean a serious breakthrough for the band and naturally we didn't want to deprive them of that. In addition, we thought it was pretty exciting to be negotiating with such a big label and financially we thought we could make a really good deal. But there was one problem we couldn't bluff our way out of. There was a contract, but there were a few points in it that we hadn't been able to fulfil. Monthly reports, sending in and translating reviews, and filling in what in our eyes was unnecessary paperwork, that sort of thing. In other words: we had met all our financial obligations, but had overlooked the administrative rigmarole.

We entered the negotiations with the same kind of nonchalance. But you'll realize that EMI started the contest very differently and with a lot more firmness. Yet the contest took an unexpected turn. After months of back-and-forth haggling about full stops, commas and other contractual twaddle, we both realized that the Dutch contract had never actually been signed. A beginner's error?

Thinking back on this, I sometimes wonder what would have happened if the contract had been signed. Would we have come out of it okay? It would probably have ended up being an expensive legal battle. We were, of course, officially negligent in the provision of information. It wouldn't have been all that strange if we'd got a hefty fine for 'illegally' releasing the music.

Fortunately, it didn't come to that. EMI suggested that as compensation for the work we'd done in the past, we could keep all the revenue we'd made over those past years. But from that point the rights would no longer belong to us. I suspect, however, that those rights never officially belonged to us anyway.

I think we could count ourselves lucky that we didn't have a signed contract. Neither side actually kept to the agreement. After all, EMI didn't have to give us anything and we weren't charged with illegally releasing music. In this case, both sides came out of it well. It's easy to say this now, of course. In fact, the band's career came to a standstill and the mega release never happened, but all the parties involved were satisfied. If the band had broken through internationally, it's probably the case that the little label in the Netherlands, which stuck its neck out to release those first three albums, would have received some further compensation for their efforts. That's also an unwritten rule in the live industry. If a booking agency does all the groundwork to build an act on the live circuit and the artist changes their agent, then it's not uncommon for the original promoter to remain on board, or at least receive some kind of compensation.

It was frustrating, however, when Nirvana's first promoter in the Netherlands lost the band to another promoter just when they were going to perform their biggest ever show in the Ahoy Arena, Rotterdam, a 10,000 capacity venue. It's true that a nice percentage of the takings would go to the little booking agency, without any risk to them at all, yet that was no more than a sticking plaster for them, because they were really fed up that they'd lost the act. But the story ended more badly still, because Nirvana's frontman, Kurt Cobain, committed suicide and the show was cancelled. Where's your contract then?

So is the answer to burn all your contracts or throw them in the waste bin unread? No, but you do need to realize that the entire industry is built on trust and relationships. Someone who only focuses on the small print isn't flexible enough for the music industry. You've got to bend with the wind, go with the flow, and get the job done together. And most of all, don't forget that you can't do everything yourself.

BEYOND YOUR OWN BACKYARD

The Greek artist Apelles, Alexander the Great's court painter, used to hide himself behind his paintings to listen undisturbed to the viewers' comments. He once heard a cobbler criticising him for not painting enough lace-holes on someone's sandal. After the artist had corrected the painting, the cobbler started fussing again, this time because a shinbone wasn't correctly depicted. Then Apelles, clearly annoyed, appeared from behind the canvas, and said the famous words: 'Cobbler, stick to your last!'

The beauty of this little story is that it might make you wonder if the shoemaker wasn't actually right. After all, the subject of the painting was in fact the shoemaker's trade. But if you look purely at the work of the artist, then the story is about how something is painted and portrayed.

You already know that music industry professionals – especially when things go wrong – always have something to say about their colleagues. But if you try to keep as much under your own control as possible, that can't happen. That's known as harvesting beyond your own backyard. In other words: promoters want to have a go at publishing and managers want to book tours, to start with the simplest examples.

The origin of this practice mainly comes from the time when record companies saw digitization dry up their revenues. The CD was past its prime, people were downloading for free en masse and prospects were awful. In short, no one had confidence anymore in the earnings model of recorded music. They were even giving away entire albums with crates of beer just to generate a bit of income. It didn't take very long for a number of clever record companies to realize that you could make something out of 'live events'. That started with a few percentages here and there, based on the idea that, after all, the company was the one investing in the artist's career. That investment was the reason there was any live income at all. But it didn't stay at a few percentages and a few companies.

Soon you couldn't find a single record deal without a live income. And then it was just a small step for record companies to set up their own booking offices or agencies. Universal wasn't unwilling to pay an eight figure sum for a British agency and in Germany booking agencies were also absorbed by the record world. The live industry responded by doing the same sort of thing: soon lots of booking agencies had their own in-house publishing team, an artist management section and a publishing company.

You definitely can't blame all those different parties: if the pie seems to be getting smaller, you'd better make sure you get more pieces. And so the 360 degree deal was born.

And that's not such a surprising idea: the more branches of the business you have in-house and can offer to an artist, the less risk you run. It means you can take your share of the artist's income from several different directions and they need just one contact point – the one-stop shop, with the added advantage that the artist doesn't have to be constantly consulting a number of different people from different disciplines.

Not such a bad business model and since you can always find good people to make it work, you're plugging a gap in the market. At least, that's what pretty much everyone in the music industry thought between 2000 and 2010. The acquisition boom had started: promoters bought radio stations, record labels bought merchandising companies, booking agencies invested in management companies. There was no end to it! And when everyone had got themselves a bit familiar with these various disciplines, then the next chapter could begin: the big artist acquisition circus.

In America they started quickly: Madonna was one of the first to sign a 360 degree deal with Live Nation. The news was announced with great fanfare: 'Is this the new business model for the music industry?' For Live Nation the deal included revenues from shows, albums, film roles, merchandise and 'other projects'. Madonna received millions as an advance, as well as getting shares in Live Nation. But just a handful of artists were acquired by various companies with this kind of 360 degree deal.

It slowly became obvious that the entire concept didn't actually work. Not so much because artists and managers seemed to come out worse – which I seriously doubt, by the way – but more because the idea of letting one single party in the industry do everything 'just didn't feel right'. After all, a record company is very good at marketing an artist because they release their music, but why would they suddenly understand touring? And concert promoters, all well and good, but what do they know about producers, album artwork and publishing contracts? In the end, only a few artists ventured into a 360 degree deal. Because even though the one-stop shop looks like a perfect model, it's not really good for negotiations. Do you want a better record deal? You don't only have to meet up with your label, but with your agent and publisher too, and they're both working for the same company. Is someone else offering you a better merchandise deal? Well, you can't go anywhere at all with it, because you're part of the total package.

But even more than being tied to one single party, it's about money. Because what makes artists and managers especially unhappy is giving income away. Why should you give away a share of the touring revenue to your label? The manager and artist could justify that in times of crisis, but now that streaming's brought the record companies back to normal, they're starting to wonder why that's still necessary. Though the company will argue that they're the ones responsible for marketing the artist, and so getting a share of the revenue from (private) performances, touring and merchandise is completely reasonable.

Many companies in the music industry are still trying to profit from activities that aren't part of their core business. Harvesting beyond your own backyard is something that's not unusual in the music industry. Not least because traditionally many things follow on from signing an artist. It's amazing to see that even at a time when most of the revenue comes from touring, record companies still control the strings far more than the promoters. But merchandising can only start when there's a tour, a tour only when there's enough music, and there's only enough music if the record label has done enough promo. The record label turns out to be – and will always be – an essential and important link in the pyramid, even though releasing music seems a lot easier these days.

Many promoters think they understand how it works and so they don't shrink from starting a label themselves. When I part-owned Alien Do God, that record label I've already mentioned (the unsigned contract story), we always kept a close eye on the finances. So much so that even buying barcodes was too big an outlay for us. Fifty barcodes easily cost 15 euros back then, so you can well imagine how stingy we were. And you've got to have barcodes, because there have to be barcodes on CDs, otherwise stores can't sell them. So we scoured the local supermarket in search of barcodes. Jars of peanut butter, pots of semi-skimmed yoghurt, packets of fennel salami slices, anything crazy enough to imagine and its barcodes ended up on our CDs. And when we signed up a Belgian act, we used the same technique, without pausing to think. It all seemed to be going swimmingly, just as before, until the drummer wanted to buy his own record in a Belgian electronics megastore. When the cashier scanned it and yelled, 'Oh my goodness, coffee filters?!' that was enough. Less than twenty-four hours later, all the CDs were back from the shops and we were sticking new barcodes on them. This time, of course, legally acquired.

We should have seen that one coming, but something I didn't expect was that as a promoter you shouldn't start your own label because it can totally work against you. Once, for example, Warner Music let us release a record by a really cool US guitar band called The Films. The idea was to increase their credibility by releasing their first album with a small, independent label. Then Warner would take the band back again for the following record. The deal was exclusively for Benelux and we always stuck to that. After all, you don't want to get in the way of your European colleagues. But the sales weren't going particularly well, and then we got a phone call from the Dutch distributor. He'd got a big order in from Asia. Well, technically speaking, the records in the Netherlands had already been sold to the distributor, at least, that's how we saw it back then. So sell them. But after the second, even bigger order, it did feel a little like cheating, so we decided not to send any more boxes of CDs to places other than Benelux.

That would all have fizzled out naturally, if it weren't for the fact that the agent then wanted to book a new tour. The band had sold less than 150 tickets per show for the first tour, but the agent insisted that we should go for venues that could take a thousand people. A phone call from the Belgian promoter, who'd got the same demand, made us suspect that the agent had gone completely mad. However, Germany and France told us that the band was going to play in small venues there. We couldn't make head or tail of it, but when the agent brought in the evidence of the sales figures, it soon became clear. The agent, manager and band all had it stated in black-and-white that the CD sales in Benelux were going brilliantly. From my position as the record label, that was something I could only confirm. But, of course, I couldn't tell them that more than 80 percent of those albums had been shipped to Asia.

In the end, the band only did one single show in a seven hundred capacity hall, and that was less than a third full. The same story in Belgium. You'll understand that no commission was earned from those shows. The band was never able to release its new album with Warner: the band decided to split up before the recording.

SHAKE & FAKE

I want to turn now to the presale phenomenon, which for me is an example of a baffling model that must have been dreamt up by the least creative people in the music industry. Releasing a *Best of* record in our current streaming era is another example. I realize that such solutions are desperately needed to keep yourself financially afloat nowadays, but sometimes I really can't understand how people let themselves be seduced by such twisted reasoning. Let's take a look at how far this has gone.

A presale is nothing more than giving people the chance to buy a ticket earlier than others who may be interested. The presale is, therefore, for the real fan! The problem is that there are various presales, and therefore also various points to choose from.

1. There's the presale exclusively for **fans of the artist**. You usually access this via the artist themself, or via a mailing list, the artist's website, or their fan club. You need to be a member or have registered to be one.

2. There's an exclusive presale for the **promoter's clients**. These could, of course, also be fans, but they need to have signed up for the promoter's mailing.

3. Then there's the presale for the **venue's contacts**. These could be fans too, but they need to have signed up for the venue's mailing list or loyalty programme.

4. The **sponsor** obviously also has a presale at their disposal. As a fan, you have to sign up for the sponsor's mailing list to get access. Lucky for you, you're going to get lots of great offers in your inbox every week from the sponsor.

5. The **media partner** usually gives exclusive access to the presale as well. For this you have to listen to the relevant radio station, watch the TV channel, or look at the website.

After these presales – or some of them – that's when the sales start for ordinary fans. Always supposing there are enough tickets and fans left, of course.

Something else that shows you can earn a nice bit of pocket money from all the peripheral stuff are the meet & greets. Once these were simply a promotional tool, but now they're being hailed by the industry as a revenue model for loss-making tours. In the early days of the music industry, record labels used this a lot to give radio stations even more exclusive content, in addition to the albums, concert tickets at home and abroad, and signed posters. A meeting with the artist was the ultimate gift a fan could win and moreover a useful way of getting fans to listen to the radio for days on end.

Those days have gone. Whole coachloads are now driven past indifferent artists simply to rake in a few more cents. You'll understand that the play on words 'shake & fake' is now more often used in the music industry than 'meet & greet'. The low point, however, must be the 'hi and goodbye' moments, when the fans are not allowed to do anything other than wave at the artist while they're leaving the concert venue in a minibus with blacked-out windows.

While the whole meet & greet story can be an excellent source of income, there are also some more or less mandatory meet & greets in the music industry itself. The employees of record companies are only too happy to shake hands on the day of the show. And on promotion days, radio DJs or influencers sometimes want to be on the photo too, in exchange for some extra promo.

Look at Blackpink, for example, the hugely popular Korean girl group – they really wanted to have their photo taken with the concert promoter. Now Korean girl groups are known for their divergent views on the music industry, and being on a photo with their concert promoter is apparently high on their to-do list. I think that some manager or another must have seen the example of Kiss – that band has to have their photo taken with the concert promoter for every show. But the promoter has to get made up and dressed in exactly the same style as the group, otherwise there'll be no show at all. Fortunately, that wasn't the case for Blackpink, because I'm sure that the ladies' costume and make-up style wouldn't have suited me at all.

CHILDREN RUIN THE MUSIC INDUSTRY

Children ruin the music industry, that's something everyone has always known. Take a good look at the successful entrepreneurs. How many kids have they brought into the world? None! How often have you heard them say they can't go out for a night because the child-minder is ill? Never! No, the people who do well in this industry keep track of everything, get enough sleep to process it all, and are always the first at the office, bright-eyed and bushy-tailed, ready to get back to work again.

And those people in the industry who do happen to have kids, end up producing a whole dynasty. The children of agents step into their parents' shoes without a second thought, while record company executives do all they can to give their little darlings a leg up. This keeps the tricks for survival in this shady world nicely in the family. Agents and promoters don't trust anyone at all, so at first the kids just help out, but in the end they're likely to become standard bearers for all the old ways. Yes, memory and know-how are transmitted without any form of progress. All very positive, of course.

But children are also the future, so we don't want them just to work in the music industry, we want them to be consumers. Which festival doesn't want 'the future' at its party? Which artist doesn't want a young and uninhibited audience? Which radio station doesn't want to show off all the latest youth crazes? Everything, in fact, has to get younger and younger, because that's how we can ensure our own future. Because the younger you get them introduced to music, the more they'll be involved with it later. Right? That's why the music industry needs to 'catch' people when they're young and make them aware of the music phenomenon and all its merits.

But kids won't get there by themselves: they need a bit of help. When they're under eighteen, they're still malleable, and if you can influence and guide them, you'll really hit gold. Boy bands, for example, have plenty of influence, far more than parents would actually like. And the music industry tries to earn its living from that influence. Yet kids are not financially interesting as such, they don't have enough money. They'll never buy anything at shows and festivals except orange squash and candyfloss. So the revenue doesn't come from the kids, but from their parents. That's because every major expense made by any kind of normal child under the age of eighteen passes through the hands of one or more parent. So when they're buying albums, concert tickets, festival admissions, someone else is watching. That's why it's very important to present great stories not only for the kids, but for the parents too.

Do you have an act at your festival that's interesting for teenagers? Well, make sure you say exactly how suitable your festival is for kids. Provide a drop-off facility, explain how much security there is, and publish your schedules in good time. Communicate with the parents and set their minds at rest, so they'll know that their offspring are in safe hands.

Of course, some parents aren't very worried about this. Some years ago the German band Tokio Hotel were going to play at a park in the Dutch city of Nijmegen. Now for shows like this it isn't unusual for fans to camp out on the pavements nights before the first notes are even played. They're not only doing this because they want to be right at the front during the show. The main reason is that it's fun and sociable. And it shows people who the really big fans are. Anyway, most fans will do this even for seated shows. In such cases you know in advance where you'll be sitting, so there's no sense in doing this if all you want is to be at the front. Nevertheless, fans will still camp for nights at the entrance, something that's always amazed me.

But for Tokio Hotel's concert in the Goffertpark it was inevitable that people would be camping out overnight because they'd sold almost 15,000 tickets, all standing. Even before the construction work started – which usually happens a week or two before the show – there was a fan in the park. Fortunately, she soon realized that she was there much too early. In fact, it's pretty difficult to choose where to camp if you don't know where the entrance or the backstage will be.

In the days before the show, more and more fans trickled in. Some parents even dropped their kids off in person a few days beforehand, even though the organizer, the city council and the police had jointly announced, several times, that staying in the park overnight was prohibited. Civil disobedience? Well no, but several parents came by every day with bags of food and drink. Have I already mentioned that we're talking about children of around fourteen years of age, spending the whole night in a park in Nijmegen without supervision or toilet facilities? I think that's crazy. But that things can get even madder is proved by the fan who passed out after three sleepless and miserable nights. The ambulance was already on the way and her parents had been phoned, when she just about managed to say: 'I can walk home by myself, because I live across the road, just twenty metres from the entrance.'

And Nijmegen isn't actually too bad in terms of night-time horrors. But this sort of thing happens all the time for shows in capitals all over the world. And such cities really aren't the best places for overnight camping. So you can imagine the relief when the doors eventually open. Finally, the fans can use the washroom, put their stuff in the cloakroom, and perhaps get something to eat. A bit of time to recover. But that's not how it goes. This is what actually happens: you rush inside the venue as quickly as possible, leaving all your stuff at the door. So it's easy enough to imagine how the rest of the night will go. Let's zoom in for a moment on the concert experience of a true fan:

> You're camping out in front of the venue with two of your friends. You've spent two nights outside in the cold, so the moment the doors look as if they're going to open, something seems to happen inside you. You feel a kind of excitement combined with a craving for the unknown. You think you know what to expect, but you can't imagine how it's going to feel. The tension rises and rises, until the doors open at last. But there's a temperature difference between outside and inside and that does something peculiar to your circulation. You haven't been eating properly these past few days, because of your nerves. You've hardly drunk anything at all, because there weren't any toilets outside. Your phone battery is almost empty, because there was nowhere to charge it. So it's not surprising that you're feeling weird before the show even starts. When the show finally begins, you and thousands of fellow fans at last see your idols. That's really them! In flesh and blood! There's a deafening scream and the band gazes out at the audience. The singer

looks straight at you and blows you a kiss. Everything turns black in front of your eyes.

A few seconds later you're carried out of the auditorium and put down on a chair with a glass of water. In the background you can vaguely hear your favourite song. And still that deafening screaming. How long were you actually unconscious?

About thirty minutes later you're in the auditorium again, but this time right at the back, with screaming fans in front of you. You try to push your way to the front, but they won't let you through. Then you find yourself a spot on the stands where you can see the whole concert perfectly. You settle down and enjoy it and after the show you start searching for your friends. Next time you'll just buy a ticket for a seat.

For most ordinary fans, who simply turn up on the afternoon of the show, shows like this are more than fantastic. And that should be your guiding principle. You're contributing to the audience's very first concert experience. They don't yet know what to expect. And so it must never be anything but the best experience of their lives. Because that's why you're doing it. Whether they're kids or adults, whether it's about concerts, videos or recorded music, every fan should be able to experience just how great it is to hear specific music for the first time. To feel how overwhelming and impressive a live show can be.

You're doing this because you want everyone, young or old, to enjoy what we hold so dear: the love of music.

ABBEY ROAD

The most amazing thing about the music industry is that everyone is always a better marketeer than the person who's been hired to do it. I do realize that there's a big difference between marketeers, publicity staff, promotion people and brand managers, but does it really matter whether you're working out a strategy or putting it into practice, or both? In the end it's about one thing: making sure that the artist gets attention. The most important thing is to be clear about what exactly should attract attention, and where and why. That's the reason why – up to now – it's been an unwritten rule that managers and record companies are the main ones to take care of the artist's promotion and marketing. I don't just mean the music, but the person (or persons) themselves, their look and everything that goes along with it. Should they wear gold shoes, for example, and should they sing on TV shows, or not?

These decisions are then communicated to the agent, the promoter, the publisher and anyone else who needs to know. Because then they can use that information in their own areas of operation. An example: Artist X is going to play their new single on a popular, national television programme. The agent can share that information with the promoter, so that they've got more ammunition to convince festivals to book the artist. And that in turn means that the local radio plugger can let radio stations know that the artist is going to appear at a lot of festivals. The more festivals the artist will play, the more people will hear them, so that means there's more reason to play the single on the radio. If it's played more frequently, that's great news for the publisher, because if they manage to get the single played on an ad, then more tickets are likely to be sold. And that's handy for the merchandiser to know, because they can then buy enough t-shirts.

Every action has its reaction, and then a further action may follow, which in its turn creates a reaction. This so-called snowball effect is pretty much the pinnacle of what an artist can achieve and to get that effect is also the most important task of the marketeer, promoter or whatever. Growth as the result of several factors that all strengthen each other, that's the key to success. Because everything revolves around marketing. Even the term 'snowball effect' is a marketing term, because if you really do roll a snowball down a mountain, it will come to a halt after a few metres because friction will stop it.

Visibility, that's what every artist needs, and, if all goes to plan, as positive as possible. But how does that actually work in the music industry? The unwritten rule for every release – whether a single, track or album – is to have a story. It doesn't matter what the story is, as long as there is one. 'We recorded the album in a turf hut, and the hut was absolutely surrounded by wasp nests. Forty-eight wasp nests full of angry wasps! And that's why you can hear all that buzzing in the background.' It doesn't matter if the story is true or not. No one needs to know that you and your brother made the recording yourselves in your bedroom. As long as you've got a story. But that's a pretty good story too, making an album with your brother in your bedroom.

Another good example: a particular album was recorded in a particular studio, with particular producers or songwriters. So what? That doesn't mean anything at all! The potential fan couldn't care less whether the record was made in The Rolling Stones' studio and produced by Jimi Hendrix and Nirvana's producers. If the songs, sound and timing don't work, it'll sound like rubbish, and the public won't buy it. Any musician at all, as long as they've got a fat enough wallet, can hire that studio and producer. The only questions you can ask the artist are 'what was it like, working with that producer?' and 'what did the studio look like?' And then you can write a great article about it.

It's better to keep other parties out of badly invented stories and to search for something that does create a feeling of authenticity. To illustrate this: Guus Meeuwis (Dutch singer), Kutless (American Christian rock) and Sudirman (the singing lawyer from Malaysia) have all recorded albums in the Abbey Road Studios. Yes, that's right. So not just The Beatles, Metallica, Muse, Adele, Lady Gaga, Oasis and thousands more. Everyone would like to be one of those Abbey Road 'greats', but I've never seen anyone mention the names of the first set of artists in their biographies.

Artists are best off telling stories like: 'I was addicted to drink, drugs and sex, but now I'm cured'; or 'I found myself in the spirituality of the future'; or 'I've got a new flame, and yeah, alright, perhaps they're the same sex as me, and you know I was so inspired by our trip to the summit of Vesuvius cos I met someone who plays the mouth harp there, and they're the person who writes all the Dalai Lama's speeches.' That gets journalists excited and then they're happy to write up pages and pages of interviews. And that's what you need for the Seven Times Tickle.

THE SEVEN TIMES TICKLE

Because that's what it's all about – the 'seven times tickle'. That is essential for gaining a degree of recognition from the general public. Because a good story has to be told many times over. Your audience has first got to be convinced about the music, and then you've got to tickle them with your story. And once they've recovered from the tickling, you've got to win them over. You need seven separate moments for that, because people apparently have to 'meet you' seven times, before you've got into their heads. So, first, people have to talk about you on the radio (not much effect, except on your friends). Second, you've got to appear on television (not much effect, except on your family). Third, some posters have to be put up across the city (again, no real effect). Then, an interview in a newspaper (things are beginning to heat up now), followed by an interview in a magazine (your granny thinks that's great and phones you to tell you) and sixth, there has to be some gossip on social media. Then, when you finally appear on television again: giga-effect! Because if you've been seen seven different times in seven different places, everyone knows who you are. That means that every link in the chain is equally important. It's the opposite of the seven year itch, when you start itching after seven years and go somewhere else. With the Seven Times Tickle, you tickle exactly seven times, and then you're in.

There are some artists who get in easily or who see it all as a piece of cake. They're already so far on in their careers that they've left the seven times rule far behind. These are the ones whose name is no longer a name, but a brand. Strangely enough, they're also the ones who are the most scared of being overtaken by others in terms of promotion. These are the artists that need to have the route between their hotel and the concert venue plastered with posters for their show or album.

I should perhaps explain. When an artist is in the country, they've got to be driven everywhere – from the hotel to the radio studio, back to the hotel, and then to a restaurant or the concert venue. Major artists aren't taken from place to place in a tour bus, but in beautiful chauffeur-driven cars. These cars have to drive through the city and so you've got some artists who like to see posters of themselves everywhere. And no, you really can't count these kinds of artists on the fingers of one hand. There are actually huge numbers of them who like to see this.

The reason? It gives the artist the idea that there's been enough promotion. I doubt that anyone has ever said to a best-selling artist: 'Actually, those posters were just put up for you – and only on the routes between your hotel, the venue and the radio station.' Artists and their managers apparently think it's important that the artist has visibility in the open air, as well as everywhere else. Even if the artist in question really doesn't need that anymore. But the idea behind this isn't actually so crazy. After all, the Seven Times Tickle doesn't have a best-before date on its packaging.

Back to the posters, because these play a bigger role in the life of an artist than you might imagine. If a show or album isn't selling, an artist will always say it's because of the posters. Whole tribes of people have banished the poster because they think they've been overtaken by online marketing. And yet there are plenty of artists who'll say: 'There weren't enough posters in the city.'

Boef, currently the most popular Dutch rapper, is known for his huge online presence. I suspect that the whole of the worldwide web was stuffed with promotion when his latest album was released. But he didn't forget the power of the poster either, because you couldn't find a single substation or bus shelter in the whole of the Netherlands without it. Old-school promotion will never vanish, no matter how much data you've got in your back pocket.

PART 4

THE ACTION

The term 'the action' refers to a specific action carried out in response to one or more observations.

What actions do you need to remember so you can survive in the music industry?

LEAVE THE DIY TO OTHERS

The DIY principle in the music industry has its origins in the punk scene. DIY, as you know, stands for 'do it yourself', and that effectively means: so you don't want to help us? We'll do it all ourselves. Because in the era when so many successful rock 'n' roll and punk bands were being born, the music industry had a surplus of music and too little time to help all those sludge bands get a serious career. A big problem, because in those days no one could predict which band was going to make it. The solution came swiftly: make choices. And when you start making choices, there has to be a residue. And the residue was made up of bands who weren't offered recording deals, or management or booker's deals either. Naturally, that wasn't the coolest story for band members to tell in their squats, so the term 'DIY' came to the rescue. Everyone who hadn't yet managed to make it in the big bad world of music grabbed hold of the concept and got cracking: they released their own records, did their own promotion, booked their own tours and of course sold their own merchandise.

And to be honest, there's not all that much wrong with DIY, at first. Most bands and artists start out like this. But as soon as it's clear that it's gone on too long, or they start bringing out their band biographies, it becomes very embarrassing. And no one is sitting around waiting for embarrassing self-written, self-published biographies of unknown DIY acts. These are the acts that are still harassing people in the music industry with their over-enthusiastic optimism for their latest album full of country-inspired marching band covers. And yes, maybe I've made that sound worse than it really is. But these kinds of bands won't ever be more than hobby bands. That's just great, go right ahead and book your own tour and release your own albums. But stop pretending you're a successful act, when everyone knows that you're still playing the punk rocker for an audience of twenty-five, because you've constantly made the wrong choices. Yes, it's a hard world, and I'm simply telling you what it's like.

In the big bad music industry it's all very simple: there is no DIY. Because the success of a band or an artist largely depends on the fact that other people think you're great. An audience, for example, that's a crucial factor in success stories. If you can't manage to get one, and the only people who put feathers in your cap for your creative endeavours are your family and a couple of friends, then maybe it is a good idea to stick the 'DIY' label onto your career. It comes across as being less embarrassing to the couple of venues who still want to book you. But the question is whether in among all that DIY there isn't something you could do that you're really good at, such as screen printing or tour management, because probably your strengths lie in a different sphere. Leave the real work to the people who are naturals, and reconcile yourself to the fact that the stage was not made for you. Then later, when you're a day-to-day manager or whatever, you can say you just rolled into that job, and that's why you're so good at it.

But the real question, of course, is: how can you tell that you haven't got talent? What tells you that no one is sitting around waiting for your act? True enough, the music industry has sometimes scared itself to death because of the so-called 'masses of missed opportunities'. Artists who weren't signed, but who did eventually become megastars. But it's actually a bit silly to talk about missed opportunities, because The Beatles did eventually get a record deal after all their rejections, and so did U2 and all the other mini and mega-artists. Nevertheless, between us we've come up with an excellent solution to such rejections: we pass people on. So if someone asks for your opinion about a particular artist, you've got three options. They're fantastic and you'll start work with them immediately. No problem at all: success and the cash comes rolling in. Possibility number two: you think they're terrible and reject them outright. The risk is that if the artist does turn out to be successful, that eats into your ego and the outside world suddenly values your opinion a lot less too. That's why the last option is the most popular and most effective. Whatever your opinion happens to be, you can say you're too busy or it's not really up your street, but you do know someone who could perhaps help the artist a little more. And then you give them the number of a colleague, competitor, friend or acquaintance. It doesn't matter exactly who, as long as you pass the buck. If success ever comes, then at any rate you were the one who set up the relationship. If nothing comes of it, no problem either, no one's spent too much time on it – not you, at least.

The art of passing the buck: if you spot that happening, as a musician, you can do two things. Stop and look for another job, or decide to do everything yourself. And that brings us back to DIY.

ANSWER IN TWO HOURS
(OR YOU'LL LOSE YOUR BIZ)

If you give people the impression you're always busy, they'll soon come to the conclusion that you're a successful entrepreneur. After all, if you spend a lot of time on something, you must know quite a bit about it. And if you're an expert, you must be good and if you're good, you must be successful. And so it all must be going well for you. That's not such a stupid idea, right? Yet I very quickly come to the conclusion that if you're so busy, you're clearly working very slowly, or else not efficiently enough. 'Busy, busy, busy. Well, if you're really so busy, you wouldn't say it three times over,' as a Dutch comedian once said. What's more important, in my opinion, is to give everyone the impression that you've got plenty to do, but you have enough time to pay some attention to new problems.

In other words, if someone spontaneously rings you up or pokes his head round the door, you should have enough time to deal with it. Projecting an image of incredible busyness (always walking round phoning other people where everyone can see you, for example) gives the impression that you've got no time to pay attention to anyone else. That means you'll get fewer conversations and fewer questions, and therefore less information. And information is exactly what you need to grow. So, do you have to talk to everyone for hours? No, of course not, that's the other extreme. You need to have just enough work to let you cut conversations off, if you're going to move on. And one of the useful tools for this is to have as many clocks as possible up on the walls. Look at what the big successful companies do. From the boss's desk, you can probably see a clock in every corner. That means they can cut meetings off without obviously looking at their watch. That gives the impression that they've got enough time for you, but they're still busy enough to move on to other things. So the next time you hear, at five to three, 'Sorry, I've got another meeting at three o'clock,' at least you'll know how it works.

Another well-known piece of advice, usually lifted from books about working efficiently, is to make sure your desk is clear at the end of the day. That's the so-called clean desk policy, something praised by all and sundry. Nowadays you could translate this to: make sure your inbox is empty by the end of the day. Or more modern still: make sure you don't have any alerts on your phone when the day ends. That gives you the feeling that everything is nice and tidy and the next day you can calmly get back to work again.

It's good advice, which you should certainly keep at the back of your mind, but of course it doesn't work in the music industry. Absolutely not if you do a lot of work with people in other time zones. To put it simply, turning off your means of communication at five o'clock in the afternoon and switching everything on again at eight o'clock in the morning is completely impossible. Unless you don't want to get any further than working in accounts or in the post room (do they still exist?). Much better advice would be: try to spread out some of your free time over the course of the day. Then if no one phones or emails you in the evening, you've struck lucky.

When you're answering emails, you need to use some subtlety. In particular, you've got to be careful with your timing. If you answer in a minute, then the other side immediately knows you're not busy and you can't have read the email very carefully. When you're answering quickly, be especially careful not to come across as being too greedy, that will only make you weaker in negotiations. Is someone sending you some new music? Then you certainly shouldn't answer within the album or track's playing time, because they'll immediately realize that you haven't spent enough time on it. No, in the digital world you have to keep your business in order through good time management. That gives people the impression that you're taking them seriously, by answering at the right time.

Have you waited more than forty-eight hours to give an answer? Then you might just as well delete the email. Is that a pity? No, because if they really do want to do business with you, you'll get a reminder anyway, or otherwise, you're just too late. Are you hoping to book a specific band that you've been offered? The tour will be fully scheduled in forty-eight hours, so if you don't respond quickly, you won't get the show. Because there are plenty of people who will answer within that time. There are countless examples of new acts who have signed with someone else because they didn't get a response, or they got it too late. When bands were still offered by fax, people used to run entire marathons to get to the fax machine the moment it started beeping out a new message. But there are plenty of examples of venue promoters who were in bed at home with a hangover and so missed getting shows, or bookers who were on holiday and so lost top artists to the competition. So remember that there are more ways of missing opportunities than through your own (lack of) instinct, intuition and expertise. You could, because of the most ridiculous circumstances, simply be too late.

Someone who really was too late in replying was the Boerderij. That's a Dutch music venue in the city of Zoetermeer. On 7 April 2009 I sent them an email, asking if the venue was available on 3 December for the Harlem Gospel Choir. For a while I wondered why there was no answer, but then, to tell the truth, I just got on with my life, without a show in Zoetermeer. But then on 17 February 2016, at 16:13, I got the following reply:

> Dear Gideon,
>
> Thanks for your email. 3rd December no longer available.
>
> Regards

As you'll realize, after seven years had passed the band wasn't available for a show in Zoetermeer either. Still, on 7 June 2017 I did offer them to the Boerderij again. I've not yet had the pleasure of receiving an answer, but I suspect I won't get one until 2024.

YOU CAN MAKE MISTAKES
(BUT NOT THE SAME ONE TWICE)

You won't find a single successful artist on this earth who in their early days wasn't rejected once or twice. By managers, labels, agents, promoters – you name it. Ask anyone in the music industry whether they've ever turned down an artist and you'll get a whole list of names in return, with the reasons why at that point there didn't seem to be much going for them. Ed Sheeran (not attractive enough), The Supremes (too young) and Missy Elliot (too plump) are just a few examples. The most spectacular example, however, must have been EMI's rejection of the black metal band Venom. Their simple 'Fuck off' sent a message that was clearer than fresh air in a glass of water.

Fortunately, all these acts were eventually signed. And all of them, most likely, with a great story. Which brings me to the famous 'spaghetti method'. Many music businesses will deny that they use it. 'No, we're not the kind of company that throws ten artists at the wall to see which ones stick.' You won't very often hear one-man businesses saying this, but in practice every entrepreneur in the music industry works in this fashion. Although no one will admit it. And don't misunderstand me, that's got nothing to do with commitment or confidence in the act. Not every act can break through. But it's rather difficult to justify to the artist that they've landed in a lottery.

It's a strange industry, in which everyone is linked together by the love of music. That makes the music industry extremely forgiving. If you make a mistake, you won't immediately be chucked out. You can get away with making incorrect sales estimates for shows or albums, a couple of times anyway. After all, everyone knows that it's a capricious world, in which even the weather can have an influence on sales. But critical errors, such as booking the wrong venue or ordering too few albums, can definitely have an impact on your career in the music industry. The first time you do that, it's still possible to ask: can this be solved? And most importantly: can you solve it yourself? Trying to get out of it or shifting it on to someone else means you'll eventually be caught out. If you solve the problem yourself, however, you'll earn back your stripes. But if you make the same mistake twice, you've probably got an ego problem and you'll soon be out.

I once booked two shows for Adele, the first two of a European tour. When I was asked if a visa was necessary for the Netherlands, I replied, with absolute conviction: 'No, of course not, no problems with visas here. We live in the Netherlands, a free country, where everyone's welcome.' But what I hadn't taken into account was that the keyboard player was from Barbados. The visa requirement for a number of countries, including Barbados, would be removed by the Dutch government in May that year. But the shows were in April! A typical case of not checking properly and misunderstanding the situation. So it was a real shock to get the phone call telling me that the keyboard player hadn't been allowed to board the plane in New York. And the second shockwave was the comment: 'And if he's not there, the show won't go ahead.' Since this show was at the start of the whole tour, they'd put a rehearsal day into the schedule. That fortunately gave me forty-eight hours, instead of twenty-four, to sort out a visa and get the keyboardist from New York to the Netherlands.

By not sleeping, and by moving heaven and earth to solve it, everything worked out in the end and the shows went on. Thanks to the government and the keyboard player, who was flexible enough to drive across New York to the Dutch consulate in the middle of the night. They were two wonderful shows. And because I immediately confessed my mistake and managed to put things right, people didn't lose faith in my abilities. But I'll never make a mistake with a visa again.

What I've learned from this and similar mistakes, is how you can actually solve the problems that crop up. People who start screaming and shouting when there's a serious error, mainly achieve the opposite effect. If there's a problem, then in the music industry the only way to put it right is to spend either time or money. People don't want to waste money and there isn't usually any time. If someone makes a mistake that has to be quickly corrected, there's no point in scolding them to death, as they're the person who'll have to put things right. Berating them or punishing them means slowing down their ability to come up with a swift solution. If someone is given enough time and peace to sort things out, you'll see that problems are solved much more quickly and efficiently.

You can make mistakes in the music industry, as long as human lives are not put at risk. And things can indeed go badly wrong sometimes, especially in events organization. Mostly because of stupid errors that could easily have been prevented. I don't mean accidents like the crush during Pearl Jam's show at Roskilde in 2000 or the thunderstorm that destroyed the Pukkelpop festival in 2011. I mean those demonstrably culpable errors that concert and festival organizers have too often made.

The Vestiville Festival in Belgium and the Fyre Festival in the Bahamas are the most recent examples, when the audience was promised a perfectly organized, luxury festival that simply wasn't the case. But these aren't too bad at all when you compare them to the Woodstock revival in 1999, the Electric Daisy Carnival and the Love Parade in 2010 or the Bloc Festival in 2011. These had serious numbers of victims, people wounded or even dead. And the list of festivals where tragedies like that have happened just goes on and on.

Of course, every festival has its own story, investigations, lawsuits and final outcomes. However, if you look at the worst cases – and I'm keeping this very succinct now – it usually comes down to the fact that too many people were allowed into clubs and festivals where fire safety was lacking. Crowd management and safety are the very first and most important aspects you must never save on. Wave goodbye to your ego in this respect and make sure you have people helping you out who really understand the subject. And don't let money be the driving factor. There are plenty of festivals and shows that lose a lot of money, but you should always make sure they're safe. You've already lost that money anyway and the best thing is to recover the costs with new shows that will pay off. Because if you really screw up one single show, then you're out. Not one promoter, agent, manager or artist will want you. And if you want to work in the music industry, they're exactly who you need.

BETTER A GOOD COPYCAT THAN A BAD INVENTOR

There are good ideas aplenty, but they stand or fall by how they're put into action. Because you can bet your bottom dollar that every brilliant idea that someone may have, has already been conceived and put into practice. Have you heard of the musician Keith Green, for example? Keith Green was a Christian singer and pianist who released his third album, *So You Wanna Go Back To Egypt*, on 7 May 1980. Because Keith thought that everyone, rich or poor, should be able to listen to his music, he decided not to make the album available through the usual sales channels. He introduced the Pay What You Want system. This means that the fans themselves can decide what they want to pay for the album: nothing at all, or much more than the traditional price. Because Keith Green had a large and loyal fanbase, this model worked brilliantly for him. Within a year and a half 200,000 albums had been packed and posted, of which 139,000 had been paid for. I did say, didn't I, that this happened in 1980?

Radiohead released its seventh album, *In Rainbows*, on 10 October 2007. The usually astute band insisted that the album should be heard by everyone, from rich to poor and in every social class. Then the band decided not to make the album available through the traditional sales channels. They used the Pay What You Want system instead. Because Radiohead has a large and loyal fanbase, this model worked brilliantly for them. But the band has never made the sales figures public.

Because Radiohead stepped across to the Pay What You Want system, it got worldwide praise for its courage and daring. This was something truly amazing, creative and innovative. But in fact they just used the same kind of trick as Keith Green. The trick that had already proved its worth twenty-seven years earlier. And when you remember that this was in the pre-internet era, which meant that it all had to happen via mail order and vouchers, you could certainly claim that it's Keith Green, not Radiohead, who should get all the credit. If only for all that effort.

Keith probably wasn't the first musician who'd made use of this concept either, and there are thousands of earlier examples of interesting ideas that failed to get fame and honour. But how bad is that? Have you ever heard of the IXI, the very first MP3 player in the world? The iPod was certainly not the first player of that kind, but it was definitely the best on the market. Or at any rate, the one with the best design and the best marketing. So although Keith Green may have been the first to come up with Pay What You Want, it's Radiohead who've put the concept on the map in our own time. And it's given them the best marketing too, no question.

Well, if you start searching the music industry for more interesting experiments and creative ideas, you won't need much time. The possibilities are so limited that such ideas are no longer seen as having been stolen. A few duets, an acoustic album, a *best of*, making a record with an orchestra, and that's it, more or less. It's not so very exciting on the live scene either. There's not much more you can do live than play with a band, and perhaps add a backing orchestra or choir. You can go acoustic or solo or intimate, the kind of thing they call *An Evening with X*, or something like that. You can try to fill the hall with more than one band, a so-called double bill show. But there's a financial disadvantage to this, because if you have your own show, you get double the fee than if you share, yet a double bill doesn't usually sell twice the number of tickets. The final possibility is playing every single number from an album on your backlist, preferably a successful one, because people seem to like that. But other than this, there aren't many more flavours on offer.

If you're a band, you could tour your own festival. The Lollapalooza festival, created by Jane Addiction's frontman, Perry Farrell, began like that. The band takes its friends and favourites on tour with them and sets up its own infrastructure. Radiohead – here we go again – once toured with its own festival marquee, which they had to set up again each time for the various shows in different countries. Mumford & Sons does a combination of these two examples with their Gentlemen of the Road Stopovers. But most artists (and business-minded managers) realize very quickly that it's a hugely expensive thing to do that's both financially unsustainable and enormously risky. That's the reason why this particular festival idea hasn't often been copied by other successful artists.

But it's in the area of song-writing and song-making that lots of ideas are pilfered. In the past, when part of another record was worked into a new song, people still talked about 'sampling'. In our own inspired era, everyone nicks indiscriminately from everyone else, although it should be noted that the usual intention is to fairly share the financial benefits. Well, perhaps not always completely fairly, but if you take a look at the credits on contemporary creations, you'll certainly see long lists of songwriters.

I don't want to claim that it's the worst thing that could happen to an artist, but being caught pinching someone else's ideas is certainly in the Top Ten of 'inconvenient blunders that can interfere with an artist's career'. Fortunately, there are plenty of ways out of this. I'll list the three most important.

1. *Deny it*
Just deny it. Say you didn't pinch the idea and add some vague story about ideas spontaneously arising at the same time in different places. And then say you've really got a lot of respect for the other artist and you'd never want to discredit them, and you've talked to each other about it, and you've found a way through. In other words: the revenue will be shared and everyone has had their five minutes of fame.

2. *Admit it*
Admit it. That's also an option, and preferably in advance. Everyone knows that Madonna pinches everything that happens to be cool at that specific moment. You've got a successful producer somewhere? Then there's a big chance they'll be credited on her next album. Madonna's *Celebration* was released just before that successful film *Exit Through the Gift Shop* made its debut. That's the one in which Banksy is followed by an artist called Mr. Brainwash. And guess what? The artwork for the album cover of Madonna's *Celebration* was created by Thierry Guetta, aka Mr. Brainwash.

3. *Keep quiet*
The third option is the easiest: you don't say anything at all. There was a scandal involving Bob Dylan – yes, the one and only singer-songwriter

Bob Dylan – because the paintings he'd made really had a lot of similarities to the work of certain renowned photographers. Now, there's always a lot to discuss with regard to similarities in music. It sounds somewhat like this, or perhaps like that, and that song is very like... well, you know. But when we're talking about images, it all becomes easier. You simply lay the paintings and photos over each other, and there's no difference at all. And what was Bob Dylan's reaction to the allegations? 'No comment.' In fact, there's been no reaction from Bob to the accusation till this very day. And no one apparently thinks that's a problem. Solved.

THE HEN WITH THE GOLDEN EGGS

Did you know that the largest theme park in the Netherlands was the first place in the world to have a surprise egg machine? One of its earliest attractions was a hen that laid golden eggs, with a little surprise for the kiddies inside. But in the original fable it wasn't a hen at all. It was a goose that laid a golden egg every day, until it was killed by the farmer, who thought there must be a large lump of gold inside it. It was the farmer's favourite goose, yet because of his greed and impatience he did something very foolish. Where have we heard that kind of thing before? The killing of the goose looks like an act of extreme laziness to me, and it's not something that would necessarily make me feel ashamed. But it's certainly very foolish. The search for the hen with the golden eggs goes ever onward. In vain.

There's still no golden formula in this industry. There's no computer that can create a perfect song and no blueprint for shaping an artist's career. I once created a booking strategy for a band that propelled them towards sold-out venues. I won't mention their name, as it's not important for the story. They started in small clubs, played at all the right festivals, and in two years' time they were getting sell-out shows in 6,000 capacity venues. We took the same route a year later, with a similar band – the same kind of music, style, looks and line-up. They even had the same record company and the same agent. Everything was the same, down to the very last detail: the same venues and festivals (even the same time slots and stages), and all in exactly the same order. There was also the same exposure on the radio and TV and in the press. We went from sold-out clubs (audiences of two hundred and fifty), to free festivals, followed by commercial festivals, and finally the bigger venues. You've already guessed it: although we'd easily sold out Paradiso for the first band, in the end we didn't sell more than a thousand tickets in total for the band we were experimenting with. One third less! Everyone in the industry thought they were great: they had hits on the radio, a fantastic team, and their tickets were selling ok.

But the experiment failed. The first band is still doing well, but you don't hear anything at all about our 'experiment band'. Result of the experiment: there is no formula. Of course, if your band plays at a big festival or has a well-known producer, there's the chance that more people will see you and notice you. But I can give you far more examples of artists this didn't work for than of artists who struck lucky. We've met those examples already: we call them 'pleasers'.

Although the above case sounds very well thought out, in practice it turns out that such tricks don't work. Of course, there are some tricks of the trade that are just standard, but you can compare these to the fact that you have to have wheels under a car. The regular stuff and the usuals.

Other than that, we just improvise. And sometimes we take a gamble. For example, I once thought it would be a good idea to book Lily Allen for a venue with a capacity of six thousand. That could go either way in terms of the sales, well or badly. The initial ticket sales were terrible, at a level where you'd say: with sales like that the audience would easily fit into Paradiso (so why did we book her for a much bigger venue?). And then you've got to improvise, especially in terms of marketing. And everyone is experimenting in that area too. Make a few badges, or dole out free condoms, and suddenly the venues sell out: hoorah! If it works, you're the king of the day. But if you trot out the same tricks for the next show, everyone thinks: that's been done already, great back then, doesn't work now. Then you come up with some other things, for a while, and then we just fall back on the old successes.

Another example: a record company releases a single by a Dutch artist with a famous international artist as part of the line-up. Brilliant! That's been done a hundred times before, of course, but if things don't go badly this time, everyone's cheering. But if you repeat the same concept six months later: it's old news. Getting a band to play with an orchestra? Wow! Everyone's talking about it. But the next one to try it? Sales are bad, and so it's a bad idea.

So how can you consciously and professionally achieve success,? Fortunately, there are plenty of books to read and plenty of courses to follow. I've had to plough through quite a few of those training courses myself, all explaining how to be a successful entrepreneur. But they all boiled down to the following set of questions:

- What is necessary for a successful project?

- What should the strategy be?

- How do you determine that strategy?

- How will we implement it?

- How can we move into the second and third phase?

- What will we do if we don't achieve our goals?

That last question is especially important. The answers to the first five questions are more or less interchangeable, as far as I'm concerned. Their main importance is to help you get your idea across to managers and bosses. Here are three examples in which we'll list answers to the first five questions:

> You need a hit song for a successful project. So you get it out on social media and the radio. You've made that decision based on previous successes with comparable artists. You're going to follow that path for the next three months and you'll involve 'the whole team'. The next single is ready and waiting, and then the final step is to release the album with a YouTube campaign, performances on major radio stations, and a promo show on television.

Or:

> You need music for a successful project. You're going to use this to expand the fanbase by playing support shows and festivals. Preferably as the support for a major international artist and playing stadiums. You've made that decision based on previous successes with comparable artists. You're going to follow that path for the next few months and then slowly work towards their own headline shows and their own

ticket sales. In the third phase that will result in sold-out venues and then a year later the act will be higher up the bill at the major festivals.

Or:

You need a song for a successful project. You're going to make sure that everyone will hear it by getting it played during lots of commercials. And you'll do a really cool campaign on TikTok, which will make the track go viral. You know this will work because in the past all the tracks in this genre have gone viral. You're going to deploy a digital street team to make that happen. Once it's a hit, you'll release an EP and tour the nightclubs. That will increase the artist's visibility, and then you'll be able to boost the artist's brand with performances on TV. Then you'll keep releasing tracks till there's enough for an album.

All really great ideas, which can be written down in two minutes. And yes, in the past such strategies did seem to work. But I could write twenty more like this. Nothing is more changeable than the music industry and if people knew exactly how it all works, we wouldn't be here. You can stop that proverbial hunt for the hen – or goose – with the golden eggs. There simply isn't any blueprint for success. And so everyone just does what they can, fortunately with plenty of enthusiasm.

But it's all about the last question, that is the most relevant one. Because what do you do if a project threatens to fail? That's the moment when you can show how flexible you can be. And it's a really important moment for you to show the artist and/or their management what you've got to offer. If everything is going well, it's impossible to make bad decisions. If everything looks as if it's going to fail, that's when it becomes clear how good you really are.

In the end, what we did to help sell Lily Allen's big show, was to hand out condoms at the Lowlands Festival, with the date of the show and the artwork of her single *Fuck You* on them. The day after Lowlands finished, her show was sold out. Was it because of the condoms, or because she'd performed at Lowlands too? Was it that ad in the music magazine, or was it the success of her new single? Was it simply momentum? To this day I have no idea which it was, and if someone does know, they're welcome to tell me. We're all just doing what we can. But believe me, 'doing what we can' at the right moment is always better than doing nothing at all.

A SATELLITE WON'T FLY

When things are going well in the music industry, one of the problems is the heavy workload. Then you have to come up with something to solve it and in most cases, I believe, the solution is to create a satellite or subsidiary company. Record labels have been the most energetic in that respect. Universal got the ball rolling with Caroline, which then became Virgin. Sony entered the market with Red Ink and EMI launched Labels, to name only a few. But how does a satellite company actually work?

A big music company – whether it's in the recording or live industry – wants to look after its early career artists, in spite of all the work pressure. Everyone will agree that this is a sensible thing to do. But the problem is that a big company is as cumbersome as an oil tanker, quite the reverse of manoeuvrable. All it can do is make big moves, and because of that it can't really pay enough attention to its young artists.

A practical example: a big record company gets in touch with the biggest radio station. But they don't have airtime to feature smaller bands. Small radio stations do, but the big company doesn't have anything to do with them anymore, because in the end the small guys will play the hits anyway. This means that you'll have to put a lot of effort into strengthening the relationship, if you want them to play the music, yet you won't make a lot from that financially. Moreover, the record label's employees are too expensive to waste their time on the 'small guys', and so they're put to work on projects that will make more profit. And the employees actually want that too, because that means they can have lunch in a fancy hotel, instead of meeting up with the small guys at a local café.

Well, swap the term 'record company' for 'promoter' or 'management agency' and you'll still have the same problem. In short, the universal answer to a heavy workload is simple: develop a satellite company.

A clever solution, but only if you follow these rules:

- The artist you sign gets the chance to develop and will receive plenty of time and attention.

- As soon as the artist makes a breakthrough, they'll step across to the parent company

A tried and tested recipe, but one that always fails. The artist who makes their first deal with a particular label or promoter generally turns out to be loyal to the people who've worked hard for them from the start. They don't actually want to be transferred to the big parent company.

Moreover, the big company doesn't just sit back and wait for a hit to emerge that they can then take over. No, they will actively keep searching for new talent. They're probably a bit more conservative in their signings, but if something with potential knocks at their door, then it's all systems go. Which is precisely what those up-and-coming acts would also like, and what they've been promised.

In practice all those satellite companies are scrapped after a few years, or they're made completely independent.

TOMORROW ALWAYS COMES

I'd now like to say a word or two to the new music professional, so I've written an encouraging letter especially for them.

Dear Newbie Music Professional,

Sometimes you'll have a project in which everything goes wrong. You'll have made every possible mistake that can be made, and your project has turned into a dragon that you simply can't fight anymore. You know for sure that it will be an enormous flop. All your money has gone down the drain and your ego's taken a tremendous battering. You feel irreparably damaged, and that's the mildest possible way of describing it. And whether it's an album release, or a tour, or a festival makes no difference at all to the outcome.

I think I should warn you: this is going to happen to you quite a few times in your career. I'd like to give you various examples of this, but I can't actually remember them anymore. The reason for this is very simple and I can only sum it up in one consoling sentence: 'Tomorrow always comes.'

And that applies whether tomorrow is 28 June, 7 October, 20 February or 26 March. And by this I don't mean birthdays or deadlines. I'm talking, for example, about release or show dates. No matter how bad the record is, or whether your show isn't selling at all, you just lick your wounds the following day and get on with the next project. We've talked a bit about the spaghetti method already. Well, you've got to see these words in the same way: 'Very annoying. Now on to the next one.'

This may sound unfeeling and of course it's awful for the artist in question, but seeing that within a year and a half or so they'll be on benefits or doing gigs in some New East republic, the best thing is to try and forget it as quickly as possible. The rest of the world will do that too, if they haven't already done so. So say goodbye, although that's always very difficult, in the music industry too. And for both sides. Because you really are doing this mainly for the music and the people. And if you've discovered some really great, talented individuals, of course you'll build up a relationship with them. You've been working together on a fantastic new project, with all the positive anticipation that brings. And during the process you grow together and get to know each other a little better too. So if the album doesn't sell, or there's no airplay, or no tickets are sold, you can always go for a second chance.

You usually do get that chance. But if it goes wrong again, or in any case doesn't go to everyone's satisfaction, then it really is time to say goodbye. And that process is also going to begin a little earlier, around the start of the second chance. Because even then there's already a bit of muttering: 'If this doesn't work, we've got no idea what will.' Or during the fine-tuning and adjustments, someone may drop the occasional funny comment: 'Well, perhaps you'd better find another label'; or: 'You're probably way too busy for us anyway, with all your big acts, since we're so small.'

At this point everyone is still beating around the bush a bit: 'Nah, of course not, we give all our artists exactly the same amount of attention'; and 'Yeah, but it's all about the music, isn't it?' Then you'll all wait for the right moment to say goodbye. And that's usually when 'something' is about to happen. In effect, an ultimatum will be issued. For example, three weeks before the start of the tour, or five weeks after the release of a single.

A great moment for farewells is when people are working on new material and the pressure is off for a while. If you get an invite for a meeting at that point, you know for sure there will be goodbyes.

I once got a lunch invitation from a Belgian act I used to book. I already had a feeling that things would turn stormy. I'd been booking them for quite some time by then, and they seemed well on their way in their career. The lunch was going to be without their manager and with just two of the five members of the band. That kind of thing already gives a signal that it's not going to be a cosy little chat. It was clear that someone was going to get the boot, and it was two against one. And because at that time I was still quite fond of my own ego, naturally I didn't want to be the loser in this competition. Luckily for me, I knew that the guys still had a particular club and a particular festival on their bucket list. In normal circumstances, I would have firmly advised them not to play there at that point in their career, because the timing was completely wrong and they just weren't ready for it yet. It could even damage their career.

On the spur of the moment, I decided that there really were other priorities than the band's career, and so I set out for Antwerp with an invitation for both the club and the festival in my pocket. Once I'd arrived at the restaurant, we chatted for twenty minutes about this and that. Just at the point that they opened their mouths to tell me what was coming, I interrupted them with the comment: 'Oh yeah, I've got a little gift for you.' The invitation was in an envelope and once they'd opened it I didn't hear a single inappropriate word. We congratulated each other, full of enthusiasm, and toasted to the good things to come.

You'll understand that it turned out later that the timing of the shows really wasn't good. They played to a half empty tent at the festival and they certainly weren't a sell-out at the club. Not long after that the band broke up, but at least they hadn't been able to break up with me. And however idiotic and childish that seems in hindsight, you do have to use tricks like that once, so you'll realize that you'll never have to use them again.

Of course, it will cost you time and courage to just go into the match knowing that no one will end up a winner. Then you'll sometimes lose an act or use all your savings on an album that doesn't sell...

Well, even then it's very simple: tomorrow always comes.

With my very best wishes,

Gideon

THE SHOW WILL GO ON, EVEN WITHOUT YOU

The show will go on, even without you, as long as you're not an artist, or a musician, or both. But there's no need for anyone else to be at the show, recording or promo gig. With the exception of Van Morrison's promoter. It used to be the case that when the singer was going to perform a show, he'd demand the presence of his promoter: 'Look, if I've got to work, he's got to work too.' In other words, if he's not there, I won't go on stage. And that's exactly what happened.

You can feel as important in the music industry as you like, but in the end music history will be written whether you're there or not. You can actually make yourself hugely important, but in the end it's the artist who has to do it, and they've got to do it alone. Managers, organizers, lawyers, record companies, you name it, are all very useful on the shopfloor. And it's also very important that they sometimes show their faces, but without them the show will still go on. When you look around you, however, as you're shoving a few people aside again, waving your nicely laminated show-off pass, you should sometimes pay attention to who really is essential to the show. The light and sound guy? No sound, no light = no show. No tour manager, stage or production manager, stage builder, stagehand, humper, backliner? No show. No security, ticket scanners, ticket sellers, washroom attendants, technicians? No show, at any rate, not with a happy audience.

But if you take away the manager, booker, promoter, record company, lawyer, publisher or accountant? No reason at all not to let the show go on. These kinds of people are only there to solve problems that don't yet exist, or perhaps never will. They're there to put the artist in the limelight, or in one way or another give them an extra boost. And, of course, to improve their relationship with other people in the music industry. But what good is a bunch of networkers when you're making a recording? The sound engineer and the backliner, the producer and the studio technicians: you need them. People who know how you, as the artist, can get the best sound out of something or how you can connect all your equipment in the most efficient way, without tripping over your cables eighty times: you need them. You don't need know-it-all managers who've never recorded a single note themselves.

No, if you really want the music industry to love you, then you'll be completely unnecessary and useless at those moments that really matter. And it's best if you realize this in advance, because that will save you a huge amount of time and misery. By the way, I don't mean to say that you shouldn't go anywhere at all. If there are places you haven't been yet, or there are some people in the venue who are worth meeting or talking to, grab the chance. But if you turn up everywhere your bands are playing, then you should perhaps start wondering how that comes across to people who actually have things to do.

There are some agents who can be found at every single showcase festival all over the world. And not just a few times either. No, they've been doing this for decades! Can you imagine? That's more than ten times each year, with an average of four days per festival, not including the travel time. That means you're wasting at least a month and half of your time each year just spotting bands. As an agent! And they no longer have the time to do the actual job on their business cards, because they're always travelling. That's not good at all. Be absent at the right moments, that'll help your career and the artist's as well.

For example, I was never at The Script's legendary show in the small upstairs venue in Paradiso. Just twenty-six tickets were sold. My motto is somewhat along the lines of: if I have to spend more on train tickets than the show's going to make, there has to be a really good reason to be there. Usually that reason is a specific manager, record company executive or agent being present, but in this case none of them were there. Local promoters think more or less the same as I do about it, so in this case they weren't there either. Only twenty-six people saw that show and I'm curious to know who they were. The show can't really have been all that legendary, because the band told me a few years later that they hadn't got much out of it either. But nevertheless you'll understand that since missing that show I haven't missed a single performance of theirs again. After a second show in Paradiso, in the sold-out Main Hall (capacity 1,500), we went straight to a sold-out Ziggo Dome (capacity 17,000).

There you have it. That very first 'legendary' show not only went on without me, but the band also became much more successful than any of us could have expected.

THE BIGGER, THE BETTER

In this line of work you sometimes meet people from the industry who have a huge reputation, certain managers, for example. There are so many positive stories about them already that you have an immense (unfounded) respect for them even before you meet. I once met a manager of that kind, and if this story was going to turn out very positively, I'd immediately tell you his name. But I do want to carry on in the music industry, so all I'll say at this point is that he's an internationally known manager with quite a few major artists in his stable.

This manager had flown over from America especially to see some of his artists perform at a festival at which, not exactly by coincidence, I happened to be backstage. One of my tasks that day, of course, was meeting that manager, something I'd never managed to do before, in all the previous years. As a rule such meetings turn out to be rather hilarious. The big boy you always pretend to be suddenly changes into a toddler who can't actually manage to reach the doorhandle, but is trying really hard. Another way of saying this: you're going to meet the king and you're doing your very best to rein in your expectations. Many people in this field of work would tackle it more boldly, of course, and simply march up to the guy and launch straight in, but not me.

After quite a bit of loitering in the Big Guy's orbit, the Great Meeting took place. I have to say, it was a very pleasant introduction. A high-level conversation, in which the famous manager clearly placed me a few steps below him. Exactly as the pyramid prescribes. These kinds of conversation always look the same. A monologue from the manager, with the promoter obediently nodding throughout. It wasn't any different this time. The manager explained his theory about the band not being active and exciting enough on stage. The band still had to work on that. Then he proudly told me that he'd promised the lead singer a financial benefit if she'd do something exciting on stage. Not in an erotic sense, by the way.

Enough nodding, it was time to see the show. And when a manager of that calibre is there, naturally you make sure that you watch the show from start to finish. No sooner said than done. And I thought it was a good show. Good sound, the audience participated really well and the lighting worked beautifully in the full sunlight. And yes, something exciting did happen, but from our spot on the festival field we could barely see it. When I went backstage at the end of the show, however, I noticed that the singer was being rolled offstage on a wheeled suitcase. She had apparently manoeuvred herself into an awkward position during the show – which, by the way, did look spectacular – and she hadn't come out of it entirely unscathed. Luckily, the TV cameras hadn't recorded the fall itself, but they did show the peculiar moment just before it. A leap across to the catwalk, but the microphone cable got in her way. The fall that followed really was stunning. The audience, however, apart from the first three rows, didn't see anything of it at all. They just thought she was doing a bit of experimental dancing.

When I spoke to the manager again, after the show, I was a little more assertive. After my words, 'Good show, but some pretty weird business on stage, right?' he repeated his monologue. He had apparently forgotten that he'd told me the whole story already, about doing something 'exciting on stage' and that he took out a twenty dollar bill and tore it in half in front of the singer's eyes. 'You'll get half of it now, and the other half after the show, if something spectacular happens.' Well, it was certainly spectacular, even if only the first three rows saw the whole thing. A costly spectacle, that meant the rest of the tour was cancelled because the singer had a bone fracture and needed six weeks of complete rest. The manager told me without blushing that he'd immediately paid her the other half of the twenty dollar bill. I didn't dare to ask him anything else, but I can imagine that the lost income from that tour did not outweigh that dollar bill.

That brings me to three highly debatable statements.

1. The bigger the manager, the better they are.

After the same manager had watched one of his other acts perform that day, he thought he should give them a detailed analysis of the show. As we've already seen, you should never be honest immediately after a show, but I believe he had other things to do that week. Fortunately, I accidentally heard the whole conversation between the singer and the manager, because I happened to be sitting next to them. This also turned into a monologue of at least forty-five minutes, and forty-three of those minutes were not worth the effort. In the remaining two minutes there was a golden rule. The singer was having some trouble with the way the show came across to a huge field full of people. The manager then gave this wise advice: 'The bigger the audience, the dumber they get.' Or: the more people you've got in front of you, the broader you have to act to get across to your audience. So then I thought: is this why that band with the brilliant record will never play to more than 250 people per city? That music is obviously far too complicated for a large target group. Could this, after all, be the deeper insight of a brilliant manager?

2. The bigger your audience, the better the music.

'The masses', or a large audience, is an entity that has its own rules of operation. The mass is the average. If you want to make your way inside the successful segment of the industry, where you need a lot of people to guarantee success, you'll have to choose the centre ground. The term for average music is 'MOR': 'middle-of-the-road', or music that sticks right to the middle. In the middle of what though? The midway point between artistically interesting, experimental lyrics and music, and crude, moronic squat-rock. Think of it as a cross between songs by The National and 2 Unlimited, and then you'll get a song by Taylor Swift. If you could combine a Frank Zappa gig with a Metallica performance, you'd undoubtedly end up with something like the stadium shows of the English rock band Muse. If you want to reach the masses, everything's got to be right in between.

So it's not surprising that we're talking about pop music here. 'Pop' stands for 'popular music': music that goes down well with the masses. So if you want to make pop music, you have to make music for the masses. And then you've got to make music that's right in the middle, because ~~a lot of people are too dumb~~ (sorry, correction), a lot of people aren't really into all the heavy meaning of a song. If you ask the masses what music they really like, they'll tell you: 'Oh, everything basically. From Coldplay to anything that's in the Charts and dance.' But then I always think: well, that isn't 'everything basically' because I know for sure that you can't get through Frank Zappa's last three albums without gagging, no matter how good they are. You just like whatever's played on the radio and what sounds easy on the ear. You just love the middle of the road.

The middle! Isn't it very boring? People aren't really stimulated there, are they? And you're never actually challenged to appreciate anything idealistic. The middle is just a faint copy of what artists actually want to get across to the mindless masses. Right? The true essence never comes across in the middle, so that's something we've got to fight, haven't we? Because the only thing that matters in the middle is money!

Yes, that's true: cash comes from the masses. It's the masses that pay back those big investments and when the masses move, you can earn a pretty penny. It costs a lot of money to make a record, to set up a tour and put it on. The more people who are willing to pay for this, the quicker you'll break even. And if things go well, you'll still have a nice bit of pocket money left. At least, after everyone else in the music industry has had their share.

3. The bigger the production, the worse the music.

It was my intention to really let rip at this statement. Because when they've had a little success some artists start getting delusions of grandeur. Nothing is big enough for them, everything has to be more exciting and more challenging. Because otherwise you won't stand out! Pure insecurity, dressed in a nicely decorated jacket. But I have to admit that I've actually seen a lot of big productions with really good music. And where the production perfectly matched what the artist was doing on stage.

So what I actually wanted to propose instead was that the bigger the production, the more the act has to hide. This is especially the case for new artists, who don't yet have enough repertoire. Or not enough hits for the whole room to roar along to. I'm talking about shows in smaller venues, not about stadiums and arenas.

If you imagine that you can win over the audience when you haven't got enough songs by taking huge stage sets on tour with you and using more than half of the show to change your costume, then you've got the wrong end of the stick. But that's not just the case for a show. Megalomaniac concept albums, double albums, and let's-have-a-video-for-every-song strategies turn out in practice to be mainly smokescreens. The real musical talent is hidden under a thick layer of whipped cream. And a lot of people can quite easily see through that. Because in the end it comes down to one thing: an audience wants to hear the music it wants to hear. And although people do want to be entertained at a concert, nothing should get too complicated. Surprises are allowed, and it's okay to have a B-stage or some kind of crazy conjuring trick during exits and entrances, but don't turn it into a musical. Then we might just as well have bought a ticket for a magic show or Les Misérables. This may sound self-evident, but you've got to let the music speak, before pulling in the whole circus. Because if the music is good, then the rest will take care of itself.

A PASS GETS YOU BACKSTAGE
(BUT PASSION GETS YOU FURTHER)

I've met quite a few of my idols, but there are many more I haven't met. I've never had my photo taken with an artist (except on three occasions). Do I regret that? Yes, because my photo album would then be full of fantastic photos of me with the biggest stars. And I'm talking here about just some of the acts I've booked myself, not even about the artists you bump into backstage every now and then.

So, was I a fan of these acts, or completely the opposite? Well, that's a strange phenomenon. When you're working with successful artists, the thought swiftly comes to mind: ten thousand fans can't be wrong. Who am I, then, to think their music is rubbish? So yes, I do enjoy the music of all the acts I book. I think it would show a lack of respect to the artists I work with if I didn't properly get to know their work. But I want to explain this a little more. In contrast to the large record companies, for example, you've got to look for your own work in the world of promoting. In other words, nothing is served up to you on a platter. You have to hunt for artists yourself, then you've got to approach managers and agents, and then hope you're one of the first to take an interest in the act. After that you have to really display your enthusiasm and come up with a step-by-step plan for the artist so that the artist, their manager and their agent will realize that you're the one they want to work with.

To summarize: as a promoter you generally step in at the point when there may be only one or two songs available. So there's no time to wait until the project is successful. It has to happen before there's any success. The same goes for signing artists with record labels: you've got to be there really early. For managers, publishers, lawyers and accountants it also works on the basis of first come, first served. Are you enthusiastic about a certain artist? Then you go for it, and if it turns out that your neighbour is just a little more enthusiastic than you, the artist will – quite rightly – go to your neighbour. All you can do then is to put your enthusiasm for great music with all your heart and soul into your work. And if you're not really into music but want to work in the music industry anyway, you've got to adopt a passion for music, because without that passion you won't get in.

And that swiftly brings me to the subject of people who think it makes them look interesting if they've got a pass to get into concerts or festivals. People who apparently need a little plastic card to show how cool they are or how far backstage they're allowed to go. People with cupboards full of laminated or plasticized passes. Or full of vinyl stickers with images of artists, dates, venues and other exciting codes. Mainly along the lines of: AAA (we've met that one already: Access All Areas), Photo (for photographers), Backstage, Working, Dressing Room, Promoter, Afterparty... these are self-explanatory, I imagine. And then the names of things that aren't allowed: No Dressing Room, No Stage, No Afterparty... Because every tour has its own system. And its own guestlist policy.

When Pearl Jam played in Rotterdam in 1992, I was queuing outside the venue with a girlfriend. Without any tickets. When Eddie Vedder walked past, to our great surprise, we rushed up to him and asked if he could get us on the guestlist. Alas, that wasn't possible, because there was no way the tour manager would believe that members of the band could make friends so quickly with the locals. A plausible reason. But in the following years, when I used to go to shows as an assistant photographer, I was never on the guestlist either. And in spite of the fact that I was the assistant photographer of 'the biggest newspaper in the Netherlands', I'd do the three-hour drive down to Pinkpop every year hoping to get in, but feeling scared stiff that I wouldn't. No one in the end dared to refuse me. But the tension wasn't pleasant. I think that's the origin of my one and only guilty pleasure. I'm going to have to confess here that I'm also someone who needs one of those plasticated passes round my neck. Just so I have the idea that I'm allowed to be there, that I belong. I should also admit that it bothers me a little less these past few years, but I can't deny it. I think this all started with that rejection from Eddie Vedder: 'You gotta be a friend to get on the guestlist, then you'll belong.'

Utter nonsense, of course.

That brings me to the wonderful world of guestlists. One of the rules of etiquette is that if you're on the guestlist, you really should drop in. Because they don't just cross your name off at the desk to make sure that someone else isn't trying to get in using the same name. No, the main purpose of those crossed-out lists is to check afterwards who didn't show up, so that you won't have to invite them again next time. Yes, invite… Because of course there are plenty of people who believe they should always be on the guestlist. Worse still: there are people who seriously don't know how to buy a ticket. They're so used to going in through the back door that they don't even know where the main entrance is.

If you can't get on a guestlist somewhere, there's one golden rule: a building or festival always has more than one entrance. And there are always several people working at every concert or festival. So use your various contacts. If one of them can't get you in, then try another. And I do have another little tip, by the way. If you go straight to the big boss and get a 'no', stop asking and just buy a ticket. It will be impossible for you to get in for free now. It's better to start a bit lower in the ranking order, and if that doesn't work, go a step higher every time. Then you'll soon find out if it's going to work. But watch out. If you try this too often, it can have a negative impact on the following times you ask for a spot. Of course, the best thing of all is when you're asked if you want to be on the guestlist. And then at a certain point you'll be in the position of being able to go to shows without being on the guestlist at all.

Assuming that you always do things correctly, or that you phone your contact first, in the worst case you could always make use of the following tip, but you do have to know the promoter's name. You walk towards the front desk, looking bored, but determined. You say your name and possibly the company you work for. Repeat it a few times if they can't find you. And if it turns out that you're not on the guestlist, then the following sentence will definitely get you in: 'I'm here for work, not fun, you know. I'd just as soon be sitting at home on the couch. And that's exactly what I'm going to do now. Are you going to explain that to your promoter?' That always works.

And if it doesn't, at least you'll be at home nice and early, lounging on that couch!

SOMEONE'S GOT TO PICK UP THE BILL

I know, a love of music doesn't pay the bills. So how do you amass wealth in the music industry? You can figure that out a little from the rules and roles. It seems you have to finance your own way up. Because the fan pays the artist, and the industry that sits between these two has to share in the meal. The higher up the pyramid you are, the more control you have over the finances, and therefore over your own income too.

- The fan pays for the ticket. That money goes to the venue. They pay the promoter, who transfers most of it to the agent. The agent sends what's left to the manager, who finally pays the artist.

- The fan pays for the album. That money goes to the retailer. They pay the record company, who transfers a chunk of it to the manager. The manager then pays the artist.

In that entire flow of transactions, everyone is trying to survive and the question is who's taking care of whom. Because ultimately the whole pyramid does manage to maintain itself. But who knows, perhaps some cracks are already appearing. Still, for the time being, with or without the pyramid, it remains a simple fact: the fan pays and the artist receives. Fair enough. What people exactly earn from the process in between remains a mystery. Because it's mainly about a passion for music and an enthusiasm for and loyalty to the industry. Being entrepreneurial may be worthy of praise, but only if you've stuck to the rules.

So follow the pyramid, my friend. Work from the bottom to the top, and don't skip any of the stages. Assume in advance that artists aren't actually colleagues who you stand and chat with at the coffee machine; and if you want to be a manager, look around and see if you've got any talented relatives or friends you can manage. Involve as many people in your projects as possible and don't try to reinvent the wheel. And if

things go wrong, learn from your mistakes and keep on developing. Go ahead and do things, for money, and begin by keeping yourself a bit in the background. Make a few good deals, share the profits, don't cheat anyone and don't try too hard to change the world. Be up-beat in your work and don't waste your time claiming to be original. And don't look before you leap, but if you do fall into a ditch, swear that that's the last time!

Keep your expectations under control, don't let your ego stand in the way, and don't expect any exceptions. Stay true to yourself, nurture real friendships and every now and then tell yourself 'Ah well, it's just work'. Put yourself under pressure, so you can laugh about it next time, and don't forget that cash comes from the masses. Although that won't necessarily deliver the best artistic results. Remember that what you show of yourself, or others, isn't in the end what the reality has to be. Try to give people unique experiences. And most of all don't forget that wealth is not to be found in money but in great stories.

Finally: try to enjoy it. Because when all's said and done, it's much nicer to pick up the bill if you've had a bit of fun from it too.

ENCORE

The future is the time that follows the past and present.

You can only predict the future after it has already happened. Which events from the past can help us understand the future?

THE PHARAOH AND THE LITTLE GREY BIRD

The music industry pyramid is very old. So old that no one really knows how long it has existed.

Once upon a time, the pyramid had a garden, and no one knew exactly how big it was. In that garden there grew a tree called the Methuselah tree, as well as the most beautiful flowers on earth. Anyone who had ever heard the slightest thing about the garden and the pyramid longed to see them. People travelled from far and wide to see such glory and magnificence at close hand.

But they didn't only travel there to view the garden. They came because a marvellous creature lived there, a little bird with the most beautiful voice in the world. The tree, the garden and the pyramid were all very lovely, but the voice of the bird was the loveliest of them all. No one could stop talking about its wonderful song. Its voice was so special, so exceptionally pure, that every day queues of people would stand outside the gate, hoping to hear the bird with their own ears. The longing to hear it was so great that wise Egyptians even organized pilgrimages to listen to it. That was because it was rumoured that listening to the bird would cure all ills. Yet no one had ever seen that bird. They had only ever heard it in the distance.

The pyramid had a pharaoh and the pharaoh was a wealthy man who had all that anyone could desire. Yet the people of his country hardly ever saw him, although there was nothing wrong with him at all. The only problem was his insomnia.

This pharaoh was not actually a recluse, but he did want to enjoy his wealth in peace and quiet and keep himself retired from public life. He had no wife or children, but he had enough places where he was welcome to spend the night. He had no idea, however, of the bird's existence. He sometimes wondered why there were always queues of people at his garden gates, yet he thought they were simply there to salute him, after a small payment, of course.

One day, after the pharaoh heard from the Roman emperor that a famous bird lived in his garden, he summoned his top civil servant and ordered him to search for it immediately. When you get a chance like that, it's best not to wait too long. The pharaoh wanted to hear the voice as well, and that very evening too. The civil servant searched for hours, until he was exhausted, and asked all the people in the garden if they knew where the bird was, but no one knew. Until at last a small boy came and told him that he always heard the bird singing when he was on his way to his music lessons. The boy himself was not very musical but understood all too well why the bird was so special.

After the civil servant and the boy had walked in the garden for an hour and a half, they reached the place where the bird always sang. 'There it is!' the boy said, and he signalled to the bird to tell it to start singing. A beautiful sound emerged from the bird's throat. But the bird itself was rather grey and it had dull-looking feathers. After a miraculously beautiful performance, the little bird flew onto the boy's shoulder. The civil servant immediately invited both of them to come that very evening to sing to the pharaoh. Naturally, the little bird, revered by so many, could not refuse, and the three of them returned to the pyramid.

Meanwhile the pharaoh had not been sitting still. The acoustics of the pyramid's most beautiful ballroom had been especially improved for the occasion. Nevertheless, the pharaoh was a little disappointed when he saw how plain the bird was in appearance. But when the beak opened, the pharaoh relaxed completely for the first time in his life, and his eyes slowly closed. He drank in the bird's velvety tones and it was exactly as if he had fallen in love once again, for the very first time in his life. And after the last note had finished, the only thing he could do was to beg to hear these sounds every night before going to sleep. For this, the pharaoh was prepared to give the ugly little grey bird all it desired.

The boy intervened and after some discussion the deal was sealed. From that moment on, the bird sang in the pyramid every day and the pharaoh slept sweetly each and every night. At last, his life was perfect, for he had everything his heart desired: all the wealth of the world and a good night's sleep. The Roman emperor was full of envy, but he also knew that you should keep your enemies on your side.

One beautiful late summer afternoon a small package was delivered to the pyramid. The pharaoh had just woken up and, without a pause for thought, he tore open the package. He was greeted by a beautiful, colourful light shining from the little box. This light was the radiance reflected from the rubies and diamonds covering the body of an exquisite metal bird. When a button was pressed the shining metal creature began to sing all the loveliest songs of the dull grey bird. In exactly the same lovely voice. The pharaoh soon ordered the two birds to sing in harmony together. But the shining bird managed to hold out far longer than the dull little bird, who soon lost its voice and so lost its job as well. He flew back into the garden, with its head hunched between its shoulders, and then no one remembered him anymore at all. From that time the pharaoh only listened to his new acquisition, which he could do whenever and for as long as he wished.

Almost a year and a half went by, and then the shining bird made a very harsh tapping noise. The pharaoh woke up with a shock and immediately understood what was happening. He tried tinkering with the mechanism himself, but decided that the job was better left to others. But the best engineers in the land could not mend the shining bird. The pharaoh was inconsolable and was close to death, due to his grief and a lack of sleep. The whole land was already preparing itself for the pharaoh's tragic end, and for his tomb, the pyramid.

At that point the boy appeared at the gate with a broad grin on his face. He had a golden cage in his hand, which he lifted up. A golden cage with dozens of little birds inside it, all with velvet throats and with songs as beautiful as their predecessor's.

And they all lived happily ever after.